ONE FOR THE MONEY:
The Sentence as a Poetic Form

A Poetry Workshop Handbook and Anthology

ONE FOR THE MONEY:
The Sentence as a Poetic Form

A Poetry Workshop Handbook and Anthology

Gary Young & Christopher Buckley

Lynx House Press | Spokane, Washington

Cover Design by Gary Young
Interior Design by Christine Holbert

Cataloging-in-Publication Data may be obtained from the Library of Congress.

ISBN 978-0-89924-126-5

LYNX HOUSE PRESS books are distributed by the University of Washington Press,
4333 Brooklyn Avenue NE, Seattle, WA 98195-9570

"Oh yes, the sentence,"
Robert Creeley once told the critic Burton Hatlen,
"that's what we call it when we put someone in jail."

CONTENTS

INTRODUCTION

One for the money,
Two for the show,
Three to get ready
And four to go.

As infants, our adventure in language begins with gurgles, ululations and repeated syllables. We sound out our first words, then phrases, and at last, complete sentences. Those first sentences may be curt, but the linguistic, intellectual and emotional distance that divides a child's howling, "Don't!", from her shouting "Don't want!", and finally "I don't want to go to bed," are great indeed, as any parent knows. With the addition of a very few words, a single utterance becomes a sentence capable of enormous nuance, subtlety and scope.

We took the title for our book from the children's rhyme, because we wanted to emphasize the fundamental nature of the poetic strategies we've highlighted here. When you're "ready to go," the sentence is a logical and most profitable way to initiate a poem. Every poem in this book is one sentence long. Teaching creative writing in high schools, colleges, universities, and at writer's conferences, we have found that the one-sentence poem provides students with the comfort of a poetic template without being prescriptive, and the freedom to explore various poetic strategies within the flexible confines of a simple, familiar structure. The sentence offers writers an elemental, syntactically discrete utterance.

When the subject and the verb are implied rather than named, a sentence may be composed of a single word, for instance, "No." With the addition of clauses (dependent, referential, declarative), or asides (digression, elaboration, emphatic repetition), the sentence may be extended to tremendous lengths.

This workbook guides writers through a range of tactics and strategies that we hope will open up new possibilities for both the beginning and the established poet. We believe strongly in teaching by example, and in addition to a series of writing exercises, this workbook offers an ample collection of poems, a diverse anthology of poetic models in a range of styles, both contemporary and traditional. We hope that our prompts will encourage and trigger poetic inspiration, but we assume that the most potent stimulus will be provided by the examples of the poems we have gathered.

CHAPTER ONE

Let the Sentence Carry You

The sentence is a vessel. When used as a poetic form, it holds an entire poetic utterance in its embrace. The one-sentence poem follows prescriptive rules of grammar, but those rules are quite elastic, and one-sentence poems reveal enormous capacity, cohesion and tensile strength. The sentence offers discipline, structure and strategy while at the same time providing a creative template that accommodates the latitude of an individual imagination. The form allows for ebb and flow, for parenthetical asides, various dependent and independent clauses or complex digressions, but the integrity of the poem remains intact; syntactical imperatives demand that the sentence cohere and work as a unit. More importantly, any poem made of a single sentence possesses an explicit coherence derived from the solidity of this most basic of syntactical units. The poet's imagination may leap between worlds, but the grammatical requirements of the sentence keep the poem focused and harnessed to the poet's vision.

The one-sentence poem is a conceit, of course; it is not a form per se, but a strategy. However, it has been used so often, by so many poets, it's easy to conceive of this strategy as a form. The simplest sentence consisting of a noun and a verb, "I see," for instance, can be extended with a slight elaboration, "I see your face," and this can serve as the engine to launch a sentence whose range is limitless:

> I see your face,
> and the moon rising over the hills
> that were charred by last summer's fires,

and I'm startled by the moonlight
as it dances over the ash,
and makes your eyes shine
even in the dark.

This strategy can be repeated using any number of words to ignite the poem:

Please . . .

Please, don't go . . .

Please, don't go
into the woods
where animals prowl,
shadows fall,
and the darkness is
deep and ravenous.

.

She left . . .

She left
before dawn . . .

She left
before dawn
when the stars
were still
bright over the mountains,
and the nighthawks
called out
as if to say goodbye.

Use these words—Yes, No, Please, Stop—to initiate a quick poem of your own, to charge and engage your imagination. Write quickly. Don't consider where the poem may go; let the sentence lead you.

CHAPTER TWO

Multum in Parvo

Multum in Parvo, much in little, might well serve as the slogan for the short one-sentence poem. The two most recognizable models of this short form are the aphorism and the epigram. Both of these forms are like icebergs: their bulk is below the surface, and the weight of their utterance is drawn by implication. The aphorism is a pithy observation that contains a general, often hard-won truth: "nothing ventured, nothing gained." The epigram originated as a Greek poetic form, and has been a staple of poets for over two thousand years. It is characterized by a concise, memorable statement, often employing a witty or ingenious ending.

Not all aphorisms or epigrams are poems, of course. However, the general character of the epigram or aphorism may drive or color a short one-sentence poem, a poem that offers a fresh understanding of experience in the immediate space of one, compact sentence. In informal jargon, the poet is giving us a new "take" on his or her subject. There is nothing new on earth, but the aphoristic or epigrammatical poem utilizes original combinations of details and images to offer a new insight, or an unpredictable response to the world.

The traditional aphorism has been a favorite tool of philosophers such as François de La Rochefoucauld, who wrote, "We are all strong enough to bear other men's misfortunes." While the aphoristic poem often employs a philosophical dialectic, its achievement is realized not only through a unique combination or juxtaposition of ideas, but by the loaded cargo of the image. Limiting the poem to a single sentence encourages concision, original imagery and discovery. The following aphoristic poems are offered as examples and inspiration.

DON'T GET YOUR HOPES UP

When they say they're praying about their decision, they've already decided.

—*Mark Jarman*

•

I would live forever if I could, but not like this.

—*Gary Young*

•

Only the dead have discovered what they cannot live without.

—*James Richardson*

•

THE FINAL WORD

Our farewells lack the plausibility of our departures.

—*Bill Knott*

•

SENTENCE

The body of a starving horse cannot forget the size it was born to.

—*Jane Hirshfield*

•

Gravity's reciprocal: the planet rises to the sparrows landing.

—*James Richardson*

•

INSOMNIA

It's 26,000 light-years to that white peony.

—*Mark Jarman*

A bit longer than the poems in the aphoristic mode, epigrams often invoke their literary lineage. The Greek poetic epigram was originally used for inscriptions on funerary ornaments. Because these inscriptions were often carved into stone, concision was a virtue. Even when elegiac, wit—sometimes biting or bleak—is a fundamental component of the epigrammatical poem.

NIOBI

By children's births, and death, I am become
So dry, that I am now mine own sad tomb.

—*John Donne*

•

Good fortune, when I hailed her recently,
Passed by me with the intimacy of shame
As one that in the dark had handled me
And could no longer recollect my name.

—*J. V. Cunningham*

•

I had gone broke, and got set to come back,
And lost, on a hot day and a fast track,
On a long shot at long odds, a black mare

By Hatred out of Envy by Despair.

—*J. V. Cunningham*

•

WINTER

I will stuff a small rag of
its sky into my pocket forever.

—*Larry Levis*

•

Every man
wages two battles:
in dreams, he struggles with God
and awake, with the sea.

—*Antonio Machado   (translated by Dennis Maloney)*

•

FOR MY ASHES

There will be no further poems from us—
it's all here now,
the collected Lummis.

—*Suzanne Lummis*

•

Relax, hummingbird, that flower isn't going anywhere.

—*Perrie Longo*

ON NOSTALGIA

To cross an ocean
You must first love the ocean
before you love the other side.

—*Suzanne Buffam*

·

METIER

The Greek fishermen do not
play on the beach and I don't
write funny poems.

—*Jack Gilbert*

·

THAT DAY

All day the cold rain fell, its clear bloodless beads
shattering all around us, as if legions of angels
were dropping their rosaries, abandoning prayer.

—*Fred Dings*

·

ON IMPEDIMENTS

Children play ball
In the crowded plaza

Not in spite of the crowd
But because of it.

—*Suzanne Buffam*

DEATH

I take you as I take the moon rising,
Darkness, black moth the light burns up in.

—*Charles Wright*

·

MAGNETIC MEMO

Decapitated,
the trout in the freezer
were yesterday swimming free
in the clear mountain stream—

heads up, pilgrim.

—*Michael Hannon*

While it may be difficult to be deeply philosophic, wise or witty upon command, the strategies utilized by the aphoristic poems above can serve as catalysts for composition. Gary Young begins his aphoristic poem with a common sentiment—the desire for immortality—but by confronting the painful realities of mortality, he reverses the reader's expectations and renounces his original desire. Perrie Longo, James Richardson, Bill Knott and Jane Hirshfield begin their poems with discrete subjects (a bird, the dead, farewells, a horse) and follow them along a surprising route. Choose a subject—an object, a concept or a state of mind—and propel it in an unpredictable direction, to an unexpected location, or to a startling image as Mark Jarman and James Richardson do. Subvert your assumptions.

The brevity of life is the predominant theme of epigrammatic poems from the Greeks to the present. Michael Hannon confronts mortality after looking at headless trout in his freezer; Jack Gilbert explains directly, with sly irony, how seriously he takes his vocation, and tangentially his realization that time is short and one must be focused. Choose an everyday object, one that may or may not be traditionally connected to notions of death, loss or grief, and use it to articulate that general theme. You may concentrate, as John Donne and Charles Wright do, on a particular image to convey the resonance and the intensity of this central emotion. Similarly, in the short space of a sentence, you might try to confront the large metaphysical quandaries (God, mortality) by comparison with a resonant physical image (the sea) as Machado does.

J. V. Cunningham's epigrams are written in regular meter and rhyme, as is John Donne's "Niobi." Traditional prosody supports the wit that is a hallmark of the epigram. Write a poem in an inherited poetic form, such as a quatrain or rhyming couplet; or compose a poem that makes use of a particular jargon, such as the horse racing vernacular in Cunningham's poem. In any case, brevity is the key.

CHAPTER THREE

Essentials

There are no tricks to writing a one-sentence poem, only the basic elements of English grammar. These elements make the sentence function, and provide for almost unlimited syntactical variation. The one-sentence poem, regardless of length, is anchored by the mechanics of subject, verb, object—syntax—which provides for not only a complete sentence, but also a complete poetic utterance. Basic grammar is essential, and if used correctly it is scaffolding that, like punctuation, disappears before the reader's eyes. Fragmented or elliptical statements rarely convey the poet's vision, but the one-sentence poem is not a grammar test. Variations in punctuation, the use of comma splices, semi-colons and em-dashes, as well as compound sentences and parenthetical asides, provide the poet with the tools to expand the latitude of composition and thought. Music, tone and pacing via line breaks, stanza breaks, or dropped lines keep the one-sentence poem from formula or uninspired repetition.

Perrie Longo's short, aphoristic poem employs simple syntax, which still suggests several levels of understanding in its use of irony and wit:

> The period misses its point.
>
> —*Perrie Longo*

Lee Herrick employs a pair of em-dashes to insert a long clause into the heart of his poem. This clause performs double-duty; it expands, elaborates and refines the subject, and effectively splices together two separate sentences: "I am one of the war fractures," and "Touch my arms and you will know." Herrick's strategy creates a more nuanced poem, one that expands his original lyric impulse. It is possible, of course, to sneak one sentence into another in many ways. In his poem "Asters," Brian Brodeur buries an independent sentence into his poem with a parenthetical aside that reinforces his poem's theme.

KOREAN POET IN CALIFORNIA

I am one of the war fractures—
a breathing fact of art,

the artifice, the brass hiss
from Isang Yun's first exiled concerto—

touch my arms and you will know.

—*Lee Herrick*

ASTERS

Not that they flourish
in hoarfrost, or flare up, bract
to bud, from blacktop
cracks (I know
none will keep), but that each
petal glisters without
meaning to, spreads its spiny
roots through chaff, unfurls
in cold clusters, tussocks
shaking, as it feeds
on ditch water, the sweet
decay found there.

—*Brian Brodeur*

Kenneth Rexroth and C.G. Hanzlicek sustain the thrust of their poems, and build tension and emotional intensity by utilizing comma splices and em–dashes to combine multiple sentences into a single, coherent statement. These poems could easily have been broken into their independent, constituent parts, but by stitching them into single sentences, the poems achieve a density, an insistence and a more powerful resolution. Notice also the way Hanzlicek's use of shorter and longer lines propels the poem forward, and serves to emphasize discrete concepts within his overall theme.

JANUARY NIGHT

late, after walking for hours on the beach,
a storm rises, with wind, rain and lightning

In front of me on my desk,
Is a typewriter and paper,
And my beautiful jagged
Crystal, larger than a skull,
And beyond, the black window,
Framing the wet and swarming
Pointillism of the city
In the night, in the valley
And spread on the distant hills
Under the rain, and beyond,
Thin rivulets of lightning
Trickling down the sky,
And all the intervening
Air wet with the fecundity
Of time and the promises
Of the earth and its routine
Annual and diurnal
Yearly and daily changeless
Motion; and once more my hours
Turn in the trough of winter
And climb towards the sun.

—Kenneth Rexroth

DISEMBARKING

Everyone had a sly smile,
A little embarrassed,
A little guilty, even a bit silly,
Because almost everyone
Thought they were going to die—
Careening take-off in a wind shear,
Collision mid-air,
Blown tires on landing,
Not to mention those terrorists
In every third seat—
And all through the flight
Regretted the stupidly undone,
The unsaid,
Mechanically ate the food
Disguised as food,
Watched the movie
No one had ever paid to see,
Listened to the attendants bowing
In schooled politeness,
Raised the shade to clouds
Parading, too near, as common clouds,
Carried on conversations
So empty they almost wished to die,
Clutched pillows stuffed
With kapok-of-comfort-lost,
Took the swaying piss of no comfort,
Flushed into the sucking wheeze,
Sat back down to no-smoking,
Seat-belt-required,
Ballooned in the whump of real earth at last,
Endured the high cicada-buzz
Of taxiing,
Grabbed the carry-on
From the overhead bin,
And emerged, wide-eyed,

Terminal,
Faced with familiar faces,
The shy smile
Almost turning to a grin.

—*C. G. Hanzlicek*

Write a poem in one sentence with simple syntax and a minimum of rhetorical flourish, a simple declaration like the first line of Lee Herrick's "Korean Poet in California." Add a parenthetical phrase as in Brian Brodeur's "Asters;" add an independent clause utilizing semi-colons or em-dashes as in Hanzlicek's "Disembarking." Keep the poem going: employ comma splices to extend your narrative, description or rhythm. Trust the sentence.

CHAPTER FOUR

Rhetoric

Rhetoric is the art of using language with persuasive effect. Classical rhetoric was originally employed to train citizens to be effective speakers in public forums and institutions like courtrooms and assemblies. In poetry, we are concerned with rhetorical phrasing that orders the language of argument, those phrases that develop logical cause and effect, and establish eloquent, compelling rhythms. Rhetorical phrasing directs the initiation and desired conclusion of an argument or complaint, and develops a logical call and response, an expectation and a resolution. This can be especially effective in the tensile elaboration of a single sentence. Practically speaking, rhetoric sets up a series of effective repetitions or this-for-that syntactical connections that sustains the reader's interest, and convinces through the force of argument or logic. Typical examples are "if/then" or "because/then" constructions, which are found in everyday language. In poetry, the most prevalent rhetorical devices are variations of anaphora or repetition, phrases repeated for emphasis throughout the body of a poem. Anaphora not only repeats phrasing that sustains a refrain, but allows for a sustained layering of theme or indictment of complaint.

if you like my poems let them

if you like my poems let them
walk in the evening, a little behind you
then people will say
"Along this road i saw a princess pass

on her way to meet her lover(it was
toward nightfall)with tall and ignorant servants."

—e.e. cummings

THE RED WHEELBARROW

so much depends
upon

a red wheel
barrow

glazed with rain
water

beside the white
chickens.

—William Carlos Williams

from OUT OF THE CRADLE ENDLESSLY ROCKING

Out of the cradle endlessly rocking,
Out of the mocking-bird's throat, the musical shuttle,
Out of the Ninth-month midnight,
Over the sterile sands and the fields beyond, where the child
leaving his bed wander'd alone, bareheaded, barefoot,
Down from the shower'd halo,
Up from the mystic play of shadows twining and twisting
     as if they were alive,
Out from the patches of briers and blackberries,
From the memories of the bird that chanted to me,
From your memories sad brother, from the fitful risings and fallings
     I heard,
From under that yellow half-moon late-risen and swollen as if with tears,

From those beginning notes of yearning and love there in the mist,
From the thousand responses of my heart never to cease,
From the myriad thence-arous'd words,
From the word stronger and more delicious than any,
From such as now they start the scene revisiting,
As a flock, twittering, rising, or overhead passing,
Borne hither, ere all eludes me, hurriedly,
A man, yet by these tears a little boy again,
Throwing myself on the sand, confronting the waves,
I, chanter of pains and joys, uniter of here and hereafter,
Taking all hints to use them, but swiftly leaping beyond them,
A reminiscence sing.

                    —*Walt Whitman*

YOU AGAIN?

You suppose because
you're you and not Keats
(who never wore a scarf)
that every stroll will end
with a piano falling from
a window, because you're
you and not a Bedouin
with blankets for a bed
and a needle through which
he'll never lead his camel
all the way to Wichita,
not Simon and his amazing
bear dancing for dinner
in Times Square as the debt
rises and the restaurants
empty, the table-top tips
contrary to all advice
a clutter of last sawbucks
though not yours, since
you're you, a friend of

Whittaker Chambers,
that faint spray of spit
whenever he spoke, though
it isn't enough to feel
callous, or was it callow,
always writing your slogan
in soap on mirrors,
"I could have been great,"
when all you've ever been is
exceptional, except today,
dancing beneath the piano
with a catcher's mitt
open above your head,
the bear lumbering against
traffic to make his date
with weight: he'll save you;
he always does.

—*James Harms*

ALIENS

How on the river the loosestrife has taken over
and how at the wedding there were spaghetti straps
and one or two swollen bellies and the judge who
married them was wearing red sneakers and he was
altogether a little pompous and how the
Guatemalans have moved into the borough
and they are picked up in front of the Flower Mart
sitting by the ice machine and there the
bargaining takes place and both sides love
light maybe because of the glittering
between the trees and locked inside the droplets,
and what the swollen river is up to and how
New York City is stealing the water and what,
with the weather events, there could be a failure
of one or more of New York's three earthen dams

or there could be a collapse of the steel tunnel
feeding the city and what the language is
they argue with and whether it's under the table
the way they get paid or there are water-marked checks
with complicated deductions and what the birds are
that eat the garbage and if a plastic milk box
turned upside down is not a good enough table
for coffee and donuts especially if the sugar
goes neatly through the holes and red plastic
makes music too and boots take the place of sneakers.

—*Gerald Stern*

AGAINST WHISTLING

How we walked for an hour hunting for the right wall
and how we kicked our feet at last while singing "Summertime,"
and one of us had a harp and one a black potato
and our feet touched the grass which from the bridge above us
must have looked heavenly which it was all fall and how
we looked like birds perched, as they say, on the wire
only there were fewer of us given our size and species
though we communed and we partook, and there was even
a kind of sound come separately and come randomly
partly from the mouth and partly from the potato
and we took at last to naming the separate grasses
which is the way it is beside walls and under wires
and some of us grew so happy we started to whistle
which is always a bad thing for beaks and for potatoes
given how in abandonment your eyes might be closed
and the horror of eagles might come down upon you.

—*Gerald Stern*

IDEAL AUDIENCE

Not scattered legions,
not a dozen from
a single region
for whom accent
matters, not a seven–
member coven,
not five shirttail
cousins; just
one free citizen—
maybe not alive
now even—who
will know with
exquisite gloom
that only we two
ever found this room.

—*Kay Ryan*

FOR THE GOOD OF THE CAUSE

As when a letter arrived from the Privy Counsel
of Edward VI to their very good Lord the Earl of Bath—
marked haste, post haste, *for lyfe, for lyfe, for lyfe,
for lyfe*—asking him to deliver up his son to the French

as a guarantee of perpetual peace; or as when
a no less urgent voice of God brought Abraham
to Mt. Moriah, knife and fire and son in hand;
or as when the beloved Son stretched bleeding
before the well-pleased Father, love forsaken;

so my father, not in the crowd but far on a knoll
away from the track, arms folded, watched me
fetch up dead last in the mile run, my best time,
and disappeared without saying a blessed word.

—*Paul Willis*

OLD MAN WATCHING A CHILD KNOCK DOWN POMEGRANATES DURING A FATA MAGANA

—Thermal, California

Leaning against the leafless
Medjool date tree, as the sun
pares his brow pink,
as the back of his throat
already feels as dry
as a strip of cotton gauze,
he sees not
pomegranates bending limbs,
an arm of palo verde swaying,
decorative granite
raised with two hands above the head,
rock-crushed pomegranates,
arils thumbed into a mouth,
rind & membrane tossed near the feet,
but instead,
severed heads tied to boughs,
a green tentacle squirming,
the shell of a desert tortoise
raised with two hands above the head,
Abel's crown split open,
red rosary beads thumbed into a mouth,
shards from a clay pot scattered near the feet,
and an oasis
where there should be concrete.

—John Olivares Espinoza

The two poems above by Gerald Stern turn on the repetition of the words "how" and "and" at the beginning of lines, sustaining the sentence with its insistent refrain. In the excerpt from "Out of the Cradle Endlessly Rocking," Walt Whitman varies the words he repeats (first "out," then "from") and creates a nearly hypnotic cadence that sustains the order of his thought. Kay Ryan makes a very effective rhetorical structure from just the use of the word "not."

Select one of the rhetorical refrains from the examples above and apply it to a subject of your own choosing. Begin a poem with a rhetorical argument, "if . . . then . . .," and see how many examples you can string together as proof of your original assertion. You may want to make a simple declaration, "If *this*," and make a list of possible consequences: "then *this,* and *this,* and *this,* and *this.*"

In the example above, Walt Whitman employs anaphora in his poem by repeating the words "out" and "from." This repetition creates a cadence that builds emotional resonance and sustains his poetic argument, while the single, extended sentence adds emphasis and cohesion to his assertions. Christopher Smart is perhaps the most notable proponent of anaphora in English poesy. The disquisition on his cat Jeoffry in *Jubilate Agno* never fails to delight, and the whole is drummed into the reader by the repetition of the word "for." Begin your poem with a preposition—Up, Down, In, On, Of, From, For, After—and repeat that preposition or prepositional phrase in most or every line to build a poem out of the serial use of your chosen word. Try employing two or more anaphora in your single sentence poem.

CHAPTER FIVE

Breaking the Rules

Cole Swensen's poem "If Land Is the Dream of It" employs a fractured syntax, which combined with an equally fractured use of space strains her poem nearly to the breaking point. The coherent intensity of the sentence's grammatical relationships allows the poem its great elasticity, and the dual indeterminacy of the poem's spatial arrangement intensifies its dramatic quality. Charles Wright's imagistic alternative to the expected narrative progression of the sentence in his poem "Scalp Mountain" demonstrates another mode of composition that courts more associative connections and illuminations.

Although many of us harbor a lingering resentment or suspicion of grammar, and still feel the trepidation we experienced while diagramming sentences for our grammar school teachers, the sentence is not, as Robert Creeley ironically suggests, a prison. Grammar, like thought, is supple and accommodating; it can stretch in unexpected and miraculous ways. The following poems stretch and even splinter syntax and grammar to exposed hidden correspondences and connections.

IF LAND IS THE DREAM OF IT

If land and the dream of it
in the palm of your hand

away there a lake
boat after boat

(and watched a boat)
and the soft sun
as light on water

(glide across the surface of the sun)
keeping its mind alive
becomes another substance altogether

of bird and hive and shore   in the series of drops
streaming off an oar   all over there   and on the other side

of the lake   the heart beats green
lost to all things   a very deep green.

—Cole Swensen

THE SENTENCE

There is that in love
which, by the syntax of,
men find women and join
their bodies to their minds

—which want so to acquire
a continuity, a place,
a demonstration that it must
be one's own sentence.

—Robert Creeley

TONIGHT

Tonight
with tongues
hanging
in the wind

I dream
of happy stoics
in a wilderness
of mad
nightingales
of the moon

an enigma
a face

about the belly
of the sea
wounded
and bloody

of stars
whimsical
and drunk

about death
an alligator
sound asleep.

—Luis Omar Salinas

SCALP MOUNTAIN

This mountain is half-hinged, an unremembered transparency
We'll come to again, and pass through, a mirror
That gives back nothing, a throatless, untouchable pane of glass in
the earth.

—Charles Wright

BEING STIRRED

in the slip   (attentiveness)
& slide   (utter laxity)

passed through—as through
a canal (with locks)—
hard passage—
after the yard is severely pruned

down to hard pan; after
      the death of beauty & fathers—our orphan-

    age—cobwebs
cleared so the weaving can begin again—

gusts of anger fill the sails, lapse,
fill the sails.

          —*Lisa Steinman*

IT SO HAPPENS

Maybe it's just me, but
my brand of muscle
is what balls
just slightly up
for stone-skipping
hole-digging
hammer-whacking,
is what doesn't
until the need arises
show itself,
and at such times,
like with wrists
crossed behind
to cradle his head
off the ground and
his arms equally tensing
beneath my weight
beneath my hands,
I go thinking
apples like I do,
because they are
like apples, perfect
for these hands,
and so happen the sun's

streaming full down
back of my head and
so happen watersound
mixing with rootsmell,
I'm saying I can see
how if maybe one were
good and one evil,
not in such a moment
might I either take
care for knowing
the difference
or knowing exactly
where these teeth
might lead me.

—*Sheila Sanderson*

STORM: FARMBOY DREAMING TO REACH THE SEA

I skiffed up rivers
and creeks of lightning
till thunder
split my covers
and down I drowned
lung by lung
to a stone
of salt the cows licked.

—*Bill Knott*

Write a poem, or take a poem you've written in response to one of the earlier prompts, and scramble your lines. Rearrange the lines in your poem to begin with the last line and end with the first; change the order of your phrases or clauses, and see what new connections are made by this skewed sequence. Don't be afraid to change your punctuation to accommodate the subsequent changes in the poem's itinerary. The rules of syntax and grammar are important—they convey meaning and the insistent rhythm of logic. However, it is possible to sometimes break a rule or "look the other way" if the end result expands signification and the associations generated by the poem. Rules of grammar can be overlooked or bent if the images and phrasing still drive the poem forward toward meaning and discovery. Sometimes it is the odd locution or the scattered syntax that gives a poem its thrust.

CHAPTER SIX

The Sentence as an Open Door: Addressing the World Directly

Many poems attempt to capture the essence of an object or event with the economy of a single utterance. The careful assembly of accurate details, the music of denotative language, can reveal a hidden importance, or wring a poetic truth from what is right in front of us. Clear description can clarify the rush and swirl of experience, distill the focus of the mind, and ground the atmosphere of the soul.

The following poems employ direct and uncomplicated diction, and at the same time avoid cliché or predictability. These poems suggest their emotional centers, and discover their meanings with subtly, with ease, and with a natural progression of syntax and diction supported by the sentence. They address the world candidly, as witnesses, without recourse to embellishment.

It is the closely observed particular, as opposed to the general, that is the hallmark of this approach. A discreet accounting keeps the poem from becoming inflated, from overreaching. The poet distills the event or object and trims the moment, the observation, to the bone. He or she concentrates on concrete detail to reveal its small, but important, realization—to open the door.

THE RUNNER

On a flat road runs the well-train'd runner,
He is lean and sinewy with muscular legs,

He is thinly clothed, he leans forward as he runs,
With lightly closed fists and arms partially rais'd.

—*Walt Whitman*

A FARM PICTURE

Through the ample open door of the peaceful country barn,
A sunlit pasture field with cattle and horses feeding,
And haze and vista, and the far horizon fading away.

—*Walt Whitman*

LOVE POEM

When we are in love, we love the grass,
And the barns, and the lightpoles,
And the small mainstreets abandoned all night.

—*Robert Bly*

THE GREAT FIGURE

Among the rain
and lights
I saw the figure 5
in gold
on a red
firetruck
moving
tense
unheeded
to gong clangs
siren howls
and wheels rumbling
through the dark city.

—*William Carlos Williams*

That winter, when we lived in the city, sirens and car alarms screamed outside our window every night, and each time they did, our son, who had lived his whole, short life in the mountains, would smile, turn his head toward the street, and say, bird.

—*Gary Young*

LITTLE SPRING POEM

The field is full of petals and singing
bees with redstart and crow
looping sky's lilac over a pond blue gold
at its edges, its surface amused
by breeze and light and the slight
movement of a solitary swan.

—*Christopher Howell*

POEM

So I find myself
trailing a forefinger through the dust
on a banister,
climbing upstairs,
where my wife
holds the instep of the moon
in her sleep.

—*Larry Levis*

THE ODDS

On the way to Ontario, just outside of La Grande, I saw a coyote standing straight and tall in the middle of a small fenced-in herd of cattle, the cows oblivious, grazing in a scattered circle around it—their calves near, their bulk perplexing the coyote, thinking about what to do next, frozen by hunger, need, and the odds against him.

—*Donald Wolff*

MORE PLEASE

Bonga Shangase, my friend, teaches in a coal mine in his homeland, Qua Zulu Natal—chalkboard schooling, so I sent reams of paper and 250 pens and his students sent back notes of thanks and asked if I could please send windows.

—*Donald Wolff*

THE REINVENTION OF HAPPINESS

I remember how I'd lie on my roof
listening to the fat violinist
below in the sleeping village
play Schubert so badly, so well.

—*Jack Gilbert*

BREASTS

This is the day the Lord has made
to write a poem about breasts

pointing high up in the twilit porches
of 1958, or falling loose facing outward

under a Mozart t-shirt
in the early Twenty-first Century,

the rustle and ticking of lingerie
nylon and silk and padded wire

rose-colored, flexible, layered and fine
on the third floor of Bloomingdale's,

its pavilion of dressing rooms platinum-colored,
curved like the hull of a ship.

—*Joseph Millar*

THE CROSSING

Not to forget that we had wooden guns once
just as the Germans did when they invaded
the Ruhr in 1936 and likewise
we abandoned wallpaper for paint
and there was an army of 500,000 monkeys
who carried wooden rifles over their heads
when they crossed the Delaware and how
the Hessians applauded and how George Washington
ordered grog for everyone there and since it
was a Christian holiday they built
the largest fire in New Jersey history
and even burned their beautiful boat whose curves
anticipated the helical waves and whose bottom
unfolded, as it were, or shot through water
something like a bottle or just skimmed
the surface like a stone and everyone sitting
stood up, not only Washington, and shouted
just above Trenton almost the shortest night
of the year and we spoke Deutsche and everyone hugged
the person to his right although the left was
not out of the question and we said, "Peace," we
always say it, the way they said it on the Rhine,
the way they said it on the Danube, and now the
Ohio, and now the Mississippi, the Batsto,
the Allegheny, hug your monkey, kiss
the nearest Romanian, kiss the nearest Greek.

—*Gerald Stern*

The poems above might be described as witnessing in detail. They examine and celebrate the smallest, simplest things: a streetlight, a farmhouse, a woman's breasts. The world in all its horror and glory is ours to embrace, and we do so whenever we address the world in our poems with open eyes and an open heart. Consider something commonplace, mundane or unremarkable—your dresser, a dirt road, a cloud; or let your mind wander to some past event—your first day of school, your wedding day, the day your broke your arm. Picture it whole in your mind, then set it down in a single, inclusive sentence.

CHAPTER SEVEN

The Sonnet

Most writers are familiar with the sonnet, a fourteen-line poem traditionally composed in iambic pentameter with varying stanza and rhyme schemes. The distilled vision and tension of the sonnet in any of its many iterations is one of the form's most salient features. However, when the sonnet is rendered on the tightened string of a single syntactical unit, the sentence, its effects are even more intense and rewarding. This can be seen in the traditional sonnets of Shakespeare, Keats and Frost, as well as in the more experimental sonnets of e.e. cummings, Bill Knott and Brad Crenshaw.

SONNET NO. 66

Tired with all these, for restful death I cry,
As, to behold desert a beggar born,
And needy nothing trimm'd in jollity,
And purest faith unhappily forsworn,
And gilded honour shamefully misplac'd,
And maiden virtue rudely strumpeted,
And right perfection wrongfully disgrac'd,
And strength by limping sway disabled,
And art made tongue-tied by authority,
And folly—doctor-like—controlling skill,
And simple truth miscall'd simplicity,
And captive good attending captain ill:

Tir'd with all these, from these would I be gone,
Save that, to die, I leave my love alone.

—*William Shakespeare*

BRIGHT STAR

Bright star! would I were steadfast as thou art—
 Not in lone splendour hung aloft the night,
And watching, with eternal lids apart,
 Like Nature's patient sleepless Eremite,
The moving waters at their priest-like task
 Of pure ablution round earth's human shores,
Or gazing on the new soft fallen mask
 Of snow upon the mountains and the moors—
No—yet still steadfast, still unchangeable,
 Pillow'd upon my fair love's ripening breast,
To feel for ever its soft fall and swell,
 Awake for ever in a sweet unrest,
Still, still to hear her tender-taken breath,
 And so live ever—or else swoon to death.

—*John Keats*

THE SILKEN TENT

She is as in a field a silken tent
At midday when the sunny summer breeze
Has dried the dew and all its ropes relent,
So that in guys it gently sways at ease,
And its supporting central cedar pole,
That is its pinnacle to heavenward
And signifies the sureness of the soul,
Seems to owe naught to any single cord,
But strictly held by none, is loosely bound
By countless silken ties of love and thought

To every thing on earth the compass round,
And only by one's going slightly taut
In the capriciousness of summer air
Is of the slightest bondage made aware.

—*Robert Frost*

MY LOVE, I AM HERE

(Eurydice in Hell)

My love, I am here, I'm waiting for you
to die and picturing the moment when
your heart stops hammering, your lips pale blue,

your fingers grow taut like the strings that won
over the gods of the dead in your bid
to bring me back, when our failed ascension

reburied me, and though I know it's bad
luck to look forward to death and I wince
at my selfish desires and wish I had

patience, I want what everyone here wants,
a lover who is willing to die for
them, because the thought of you alive haunts

me and I'm starting to fade and I fear
if you don't come soon I will disappear.

—*Lauren Watel*

COMING TO GRIEF

When I think of falling insipidly through the ice,
how I pulled like poor Peter at Jesus' skirts,
clawed at the parts of the pond that still worked,

past the hen's teeth of ice, each breath coming out like a birth,
till I floated far-flung on the sled of another world,
I wonder, had I ended, bobbing, bloated, a buoy
on the dumb underside, wordless balloon, piñata from hell,
if my heart would have risen like a cold desperado
past my flailing third flash of family and friends,
my boots full of fish, my eyes two coronas, absolute moons,
my helicopter heart lifting up through the cracks
to drift through the trees, the silver lace,
to your window this night, to your halcyon face,
to the home in your heart, to my resting place.

—*John Hodgen*

KEYS IN HIS HAND

Sometimes a man home late
is steps away from his door
when suddenly out of the dark
a passing car lights up a window

just in front of him so the room
behind it is thrust into such
a semblance of clarity that once
again he sees why we see only

with glimpses like this, with
happen flashes as avid as this,

but always the lane's corner takes
that revelation past before
he even resumes the posture
of his intent to enter, to live there.

—*Bill Knott*

SONNETS—UNREALITIES

III

it is at moments after i have dreamed
of the rare entertainment of your eyes,
when (being fool to fancy) i have deemed

with your peculiar mouth my heart made wise;
at moments when the glassy darkness holds

the genuine apparition of your smile
(it was through tears always) and silence moulds
such strangeness as was mine a little while;

moments when my once more illustrious arms
are filled with fascination, when my breast
wears the intolerant brightness of your charms:

one pierced moment whiter than the rest
—turning from the tremendous lie of sleep
i watch the roses of the day grow deep.

—*e.e.cummings*

MUSCATEL SONNET

You follow the old man
who hauls a plastic garbage bag
sloping up the street—
feel its drag and clank
tugging like ballast, a hard
pull backward that you must pull
against in order to drag
your sorrows along the path
of least resistance, scrap metal feet

chugging toward all that can be
hoped for, a clear night
for Jupiter's blessing, a bag
of smashed cans too full for regret,
a warm spot in your gut.

—Dixie Salazar

FROM *MEDEA*

From this instant she is rendered up by all the angels she has served to
the oblivion of her dementia, and tendered by the holy nurses called to
see to her abominations, wearing gloves and walking circumspectly, not
as fools, but as wise to take precautions of the sort of any middle class
or prudent citizen who secretly perverts their common sense to touch
her pestilential sores and learn about the times she served her children
to her second husband, girl and boy, on this little spot of earth—whose
appetites consumed him, but ate her first.

—Brad Crenshaw

Most of us have written traditional sonnets, either Shakespearean ("Son-
net No. 66" and "Bright Star") or Petrarchan ("The Silken Tent"), but
the form is extraordinarily elastic, and as you can see from the examples
above, the syntactical vehicle of a single sentence accommodates and pro-
pels it to an even swifter, dynamic resolution. Don't let the exigencies
of the form intimidate you. Choose one of the traditional sonnet forms,
and consider it a guide or suggestion rather than a strict, prescriptive
construction. Or if rhyming does not come naturally, you may want to
try Bouts-Rimés, an old French writing game in which the poet adopts
the end-rhymes of a favorite sonnet, and writes a new sonnet utilizing the
rhymes of the chosen poem. Let the grammatical engine of the sentence
guide your phrasing as you negotiate the demands of the form.

Don't be afraid to experiment. e.e. cummings shuffles the typical stan-
zaic structure in his one-sentence sonnet, and in her "Muscatel Sonnet,"
Dixie Salazar eschews both rhyme and traditional meter to create a poem

that reinforces her gritty vision of urban redemption. In each poem, the sentence supports the lyric trajectory.

The poem that least resembles a traditional sonnet in our selection, Brad Crenshaw's "Medea," is in fact a strict Shakespearean sonnet, which has been rendered as a prose poem. While Crenshaw used the sonnet form to structure and guide his poetic composition, he preferred to erase the poem's formal appearance in order to allow a more comfortable and natural voice to emerge. Take a traditional sonnet (or something close) and reconstitute it as a prose poem. Notice how your end rhymes soften and turn into internal rhymes or assonance, steadying the voice speaking in the poem.

CHAPTER EIGHT

Transformation of the Everyday

M ost poets have day jobs. When poets are asked what they most need, a significant number will say (after initially responding with "a winning lottery ticket" or "a trust fund"), "Time to stare out the window." Poets need time to respond to the smallest changes in the world around them; they need the opportunity to find the extraordinary locked in the ordinary.

As with Blake's "world in a grain of sand," the full apprehension of even the simplest experience can be an invitation to the mysteries of the world. To even approach them, one must pay close attention to the elements of daily life, no mater how mundane or common. Looking through the veneer of the ordinary, the poet discovers the fingerprints of the infinite.

AH! SUN-FLOWER

Ah Sun-flower! weary of time,
Who countest the steps of the Sun:
Seeking after that sweet golden clime
Where the travellers journey is done;

Where the Youth pined away with desire,
And the pale Virgin shrouded in snow:
Arise from their graves and aspire,
Where my Sun-flower wishes to go.

—*William Blake*

DEAR LITTLE BOY

in lipstick and nail enamel
ears pierced, mouth pursed in a perpetual kiss
promised to a heads or tails cruiser
i hear your mother works the docks in Frisco
and your father's home anxious
waiting to count your
night's take.

—*Wanda Coleman*

OHIO

Looking across a field
at a stand of trees
—more than a windbreak
less than a forest—
is pretty much all
the view we have

in summer it's lush
in winter it gets
down to two or
three tones for
variety
there might be
an unpainted barn
water patches
a transmission tower

yet there's a lot
to see
you could sit
all day on the rusty
seat of a harrow
with that view before you
and all the sorrows

this earth has seen
sees now will see
could pass through
you like a long
mad bolt of lightning
leaving you drained
and shaken
still
at dusk
the field would be
the same and the growing
shadows of the trees
would cross it toward you
until you rose your heart
pounding with joy and walked
gladly through the weeds
and toward the trees.

—*David Young*

COOKING LESSON

Hands only,
my grandmother instructs,
and thrusts hers, rivered
with purple veins—confident
only when cooking—into
the bowl of jang-jorim, kneading
the pepper and garlic
with the thread-thin strands of beef,
and tells me in Korea garlic bulbs
are large as fists, which sounds
to me like an image from a child's story
as I stand behind her, looking
at my hands, holding a wooden spoon,
trying to learn a memory secondhand.

—*Christine Kitano*

FIVE

Home from kindergarten, I'd see
my mother on her knees, arms spread
for me, I'd run to her through the green
yards, laughing and running right past her,
Oh house, I've missed you so!

—*Jan Bottiglieri*

UNRELENTING

I was a boy at summer camp, and a shaggy-haired Vietnam vet told
us a story around the campfire about a dead baby in a village, burned
head-to-toe and portioned next to a pile of spilled rice, and insisted the
child's ghost had followed him home, then waved shyly with his missing
hand—did we see?—it was in the trees, and though I had no nightmares,
I dreamed of flying across a dark ocean toward a glistening shore, and in
the morning woke to shame, having wet my bunk.

—*Derek McKown*

OCTOBER IN KANSAS

—for Emma, when she was ten

Beneath every tree
tangles of gold leaf,
rubies, and flat orange hands
wave in the new cold, even after dark
you can hear this brightness
teasing the wind
and the wind muttering, walking in circles
on its large, invisible feet.

—*Christopher Howell*

ANOTHER BIRTHDAY POEM

"I'd rather wash dishes drunk
than eat off paper plates,"
you said, and I swore one day
I'd use those lines in a poem,
but look, it's two years later,
we're that much older, closer
to the end and each other
though geography might object,
still washing dishes
a little less drunk than we'd like
but drunk enough on sunlight
whose lethal influence is inescapable
even when it rains, like time
flooding down lifelike
over our aching roofs
which need to be replaced
but meanwhile we will place
our dirty plates up there
all winter long to be rinsed
by weather that
insists on drumming its
rituals into our skulls,
its rhythms redolent of calypso,
its singular power to
wash out roads and sweep us into creeks
unannounced, like breeze
in the kiwi, which needs
a haircut, and the nightshade
fruit that needs picking
while I procrastinate to
celebrate your birth,
late but so what.

—*Stephen Kessler*

THE NEW DOG

Into the gravity of my life,
the serious ceremonies
of polish and paper
and pen, has come

this manic animal
whose innocent disruptions
make nonsense
of my old simplicities—

as if I needed him
to prove again that after
all the careful planning,
anything can happen.

—*Linda Pastan*

ETERNITY AT ZAK'S CAR WASH

Set in neutral, the station wagon rolled
Between the rails, was lathered and rinsed,
Then blown dry by a howling siren,
The mirrors wiped of soapy tears
By a Mexican smiling a gold grille,
And finally frisked by a vacuum—
The French Fries on the mats standing up
Soldier straight, some quivering,
Before they flew up the hose,
Rattling toward the end of a clotted tunnel.

—*Gary Soto*

IF WE STILL BELIEVED THE WORLD WAS FLAT

Instead of tending
    to my children's runny noses
        and letting out my husband's waistband,
            I would find a boat, cobalt blue, the color of rest, and

slowly,
like a barnacled beast who knows nothing
but to go, to go, to lay eggs
and abandon her nest
to the wet noses
of curious
dogs,

      I would sail with eyes cool
        upon the horizon, tight as an empty
           clothesline; and beyond, the nothingness
                dark as the house-grave of the loggerhead

who lugs
her carapace shaggy with sea-moss
and would go far, so far,
in order
never to
come
back.

            —Rhett Iseman Trull

THE MAD WOMAN'S HARP

Before she left she set it there
on the east bank of the Kings,
just below the Rio Vista Treatment Center
and leaned it against the thick, white oak
and slotted its pedals in mud for stability

for all the others like her to easily find
beside the fog-cooled boulder
overlooking the occasional German Brown
jumping for grasshoppers and flies,
to wait for heaven to plant seeds
in their mad fingers so they would match
their own music to the glide of the hawk
veering through the silver framed day
and the wild swan's coast to the notes
of driftwood and nude pianos
in the airy grace of leaves sweeping
through space and never touching earth
inducing the sun to cover its face
behind the Calaveras pine
just long enough for it to catch its breath.

—*Jon Veinberg*

DURING THE RAINS

Driving through the rain this morning, I saw two men walking in a
lake that a week ago was pasture, two men ankle deep in the shallows,
stringing barbed wire and trying to hammer fence posts into water, one
holding a stake, the other with ferocity swinging a maul, horses standing
around them, miserable, cattle up to their hocks in water, the Carson
plain in flood, fields runneled with gills and freshets, culverts washed out,
hillsides loosening, slipping, everything disintegrating, coming apart, the
dead bear I found yesterday below Loope Canyon, skeleton unlocking,
carcass sodden, dissolving in rain, and now this morning those two men
near Miden driving stakes into water, stringing wire across a lake, trying
to keep it all in, trying to keep it whole, driving these words into the
page, as if I could lash the body together, not let anything come apart,
dissolve, wash away.

—*Joseph Stroud*

One way to move beyond the physical to the metaphysical, from the ordinary to the extraordinary, is to annunciate the larger conceit in the title, and have it work against the narrative body of your poem. Gary Soto turns his poem on the word "Eternity," the first word in his title, pitting the conceptual against the actual. Soto resolves the poem by identifying the emblematic as well as the concrete detail of the tunnel at the end of his poem. Try a short narrative poem whose title, like Soto's, names a concept that expands or telescopes the essential facts and plot of the poem and turns them toward a larger, more resonant idea.

Discovering myth in familiar landscapes can transform concrete detail and imagery, and produce a poem that adds up to more than the sum of its parts. Look again at Jon Veinberg's "The Mad Woman's Harp," and see how he allows his imagination and the ancient texture of myth to transform a very specific and well-known local landmark. Select a locale you know well, and imagine it as a mythic place, the setting of some ancient tale. See if the impulse of the sentence can aid you in discovering more there than first meets the eye.

The instinct of a turtle leads Rhett Iseman Trull to an introspective theme that transcends birth and death. Notice her carefully arranged stanzas, and listen to her command of syntax as every word lines up to take its place to make meaning. Consider some cycles or basic processes in nature—the seasons, migrations, aging—that might lead you to a larger theme, an elevated or expansive consciousness.

Place is always important in poetry. David Young walks through the landscape of Ohio, and that exterior landscape reveals an interior, emotional landscape. Young's short lines and the syncopated syntax of his sentence keep his poem moving, though the mood is pensive and reflective. We walk with the poet and discover the sorrows inherent in his very concrete vision. Nature often seems to mirror the topography of our inner lives. Think of a place that holds a special meaning to you, and write about it as if it was an interior space, a geography of the soul.

CHAPTER NINE

Art and Creation

Ekphrastic poetry, poetry inspired by or responding to another work of art, has been a staple of poets for centuries. Most of us are familiar with Keats' "Ode on a Grecian Urn." and Brueghel's "Icarus Falling" inspired marvelous poems by both W. C. Williams and W. H. Auden. Ekphrasis was common among Renaissance poets, and the strategy was used frequently by the Pre-Raphaelites and Romantic poets as well. Compelling poems have been written about photographs, sculptures, films, dance and music, and poets have also responded to the exercise of craft and composition in one medium or another.

WORD OVER ALL, BEAUTIFUL AS SKY

Chagall Windows, Mainz

The tall doors I thought bolted
gave way and swung with such well-oiled ease
I lurched forward a step,
and stunned, stood under the vault,
breathed a blue as mild as the arms that held Tobias,

a blue that glows at the core of silver,
blue of comets arcing the zenith,
blue glint of armor the angels wear on errands to earth,
and in no way I could think of was that blue
a lie, a pretty delusion, a hoped-for answer

to the question we keep asking empty space
that never says anything in reply,
though that blue is the divine itself
and I believe in no such thing,
besides the necessity of it

struggling toward us through glass
high on the walls of chancel and nave
twice reduced to ruins by war,
the blue of reconciliation,
word over all, beautiful as sky,

blue a man, not a god,
conceived in his final year,
an old man, full to the brim, reconciled
despite the farce that deformed entire peoples
and scattered us like pieces of broken bell,

that man, even as he fell into oblivion,
fell without a trace of regret,
this radiance pouring from his mind,
blue returning from its exile
in the absolute zero of the void, what is possible

always, asserting its fidelity to our world.

—*David Axelrod*

VISITATION

Nightfall,
the paper spread before you,
your hands discovering its texture
in charcoal deepening to the circumference
of shade and light, the lines'
swirl and smudge: departure,
blur of rain at the window;

the unexpected blue beyond
opens through the boundaries
of paper, through your hands
which settle into its heavy surface
and hold it there.

—*Timothy Sheehan*

DOCUMENT ATTRIBUTED TO GOYA

I can hear them, Maja, I know
what you're thinking—how many
years I've been *sordo,* since the fever
of '92, that bonfire that consumed
sound, waves of nausea, double-
vision, you my most beloved
double, nights I turn to your arms,
not there, my profane, my naked

one holding the gaze of all Spain,
because, yes, I spared them nothing,
the Inquisitor with his soft hands
at my threshold, blinking behind
thick lenses, the knock at the door,
when it came, reverberated
up through my feet, sound rising
from the earth for us, the deaf,
and in dreams, but lately, yes,
in this small room of the soul
where they've lodged me—

spiders—most assuredly awake
& when I turn my head—gone,
gradually coming in from *rincones,*
not disappearing, woman-faces, eyes
open enquiring, they are preening
themselves, even now as I write

this, tiny, fastidious, and their sound
is ropy like saliva, like rough silk

a feminine rasping, they meet
my gaze full-on the way you
used to, bold and demure
as though you were not
unclothed, the tallow
of your thighs, your breasts
white mounds in my eyes,
Maja, te recuerdo, I am
your
Francisco

      —Marsha de la O

WHITE SPACE

There was no music
on the written page

before white space
intervened between

words and sentences,
lines and stanzas—

and words were grateful
because it sometimes

lifted and carried them
when they leaned

into it, and the better
they got to know it

the more they admired
its immaculate condition—

which made them feel
all spotty, so they hoped

if they rubbed elbows
with it long enough,

something of that purity
would rub off on them,

they began to aspire
to music's wordlessness,

since everything they did
was meant to point

to something beyond
themselves anyway—

maybe if they slowly dis-
appeared into the white space

no one would miss them,
they thought, in a fit

of longing and self-pity,
maybe they should retire

and leave the stage
to music's unblemished

perfection—but as they were
clambering down

they saw that without them
white space was nothing,
their part in things was
modest but crucial—to

hang around outside
the jazz joint that looks like

a hole in the wall,
urging passersby to stop and listen:

*there isn't much to see,
but the music is really something.*

—*Sharon Bryan*

FOR GWANGHYUN'S LIBRARY

Even as the moon descends into the well, the jar inside the well, it reveals
the great emptiness that is the jar summoning others who will come after
the fact of the jar descends inside the moon.

—*Jennifer Kwan Dobbs*

ZEN BRUSH

—it was like holding a piece of straw
above an endless ocean

—*Monk Song Yoon*

I am dreaming of fields
before the harvest

where everything moves
to sun and wind

wave after wave
a sea of golden yellow

embracing the ground
with seeded eyes

what rain will fatten
this piece of straw

which warm beam
of morning light

with a single stem
I wake once more

to know how far
I've come to taste you.

—Amy Uyematsu

THE WRITER

She has fallen, in the blue-ish glow of the nightlight,
Asleep, her face pressed in the carpet, her hand
Still curled around the fat yellow pencil
She has used to write my name on the blank page
Of her spiral notebook: not *Mom,* but *Kate,*
The K twirling, vinelike, umbilical, funicular,
Down to a nest of scribbles within which
She must have sought the outlines of the four
Different letters that compose her name—the name
That is hers alone—for which she alone
must take responsibility—but which she cannot
yet discern within the clamor of her text.

—Kate Daniels

IDENTITY THEFT

I write a name out of the past, one
you thought I forgot, I write
slowly with my one magical
forefinger on the remembered slate
of the surface of a still pond,
forming each letter so slowly and
gravely, that now these eleven letters
are the life of one man broken down
into the separate explosions
of tongue on teeth so that he's here
as you are, as I am, in name only.

—*Philip Levine*

The poems above offer a wide range of models and subjects, and suggest a multitude of possible strategies for your own ekphrastic poems. Inspired by Marc Chagall's stained glass windows, David Axelrod investigates not only the windows themselves, but uses this work of art as a springboard into a metaphysical inquiry. Marsha de la O begins her poem with a well-known painting by Goya, describes the work, but raises the strategic ante by taking on the persona of the painter. Amy Uyematsu, Kate Daniels and Timothy Sheehan write about the art of the calligrapher, the writer and the visual artist, respectively. In the final example, Philip Levine uses the physical act of writing to ignite an elegiac memory.

Everyone has a favorite painting, movie, sculpture, symphony or blues song. One of the poems above may inspire a quick start to your own ekphrastic poem—on a painting, photograph or other creative work. Jot a short list of details or images you best remember from your selected work of art. If you have the work in front of you, reflect not only on its subject and form, but also on its emotional effect on you, its echo. In your poem, you become a conduit for the work itself, for the expanded imagination of the artist, and for the potential for the work to resonate in others. You may decide to simply describe a work of art; imaginatively participate in the creation of a particular artwork; or perhaps even place yourself in a painting, ballet or artist's studio. Writing your poem as a single sentence will insure that you choose the most essential, salient and emblematic details.

No matter which subject a poet selects to respond to, it is important to remember in all cases that the poet's aesthetic task is to do more than simply describe what is seen (or heard). Locate yourself in relation to the work of art. The poem should move beyond the avowed subject to a fresh understanding or realization.

CHAPTER TEN

Love

There is no subject more common to poetry than love. It is also the subject most burdened with cliché, sentimentality and predictable emotional context. It is one of the most difficult subjects to address in fresh, emotionally honest and original language, which is why a good love poem still has the ability to move us—to tears, to laughter, to passion or to wonder.

The one-sentence poem seems particularly well suited to the love poem. This embracing, inclusive form mirrors our hunger to connect everything to the object of our desire. The poem, like a lover, becomes the world. Polly Bee's poem "The Basque Hotel Noriega" races breathlessly through the initial thrill and adventures of a new love affair, and we follow the narrator through the maturing relationship until its startling, heartbreaking conclusion.

Yeats makes a very conscious decision to connect the three stanzas of his poem "When You Are Old." Each stanza could stand grammatically as an independent sentence, but by connecting each section of the poem with a semicolon, Yeats stitches the past, the present and the future of a love affair into a single, interconnected unit.

THE BASQUE HOTEL NORIEGA

Jane serves me crackers & cheddar in bed & Chablis in a cup at the Blue Bird Motel in Cambria, night one of our two-day getaway, she wise to the ways of women in love, me new to the game, no clue of foreplay or fun & scared to eat crackers & cheese in bed after marriage for years to a bim-bam/roll-over-go-to-sleep-man & the next day, Sunday, 11:00 a.m., I can't believe we're drinking wine on the balcony of Santa Maria Inn overlooking the park, me who was taught decent folks—those of us from Ohio—go to church Sundays, & later that day in Bakersfield at the Basque Hotel Noriega, we crowd into a bar with dozens of others 'til 5 p.m. when they let us all into a cavernous room filled with laughter & chatter to sit at long tables with strangers and platters of meats & potatoes, salads & sauces & I can't believe it is me sitting there with her & reach for a carafe of cabernet to fill her glass but she shakes her head, "Only men pour for the ladies "softly she says, & the man next to her fills her glass & mine & I watch how she swirls, sniffs, tongue-kisses the liquid, savors each sip & I do what she does & together we savor & sip and kiss, & for years we live like this & then she dies, leaves me no wine, no crumbs of crackers & cheese in bed, no one to teach me the etiquette of death.

—*Polly Bee*

WHEN YOU ARE OLD

When you are old and grey and full of sleep,
And nodding by the fire, take down this book,
And slowly read, and dream of the soft look
Your eyes had once, and of their shadows deep;

How many loved your moments of glad grace,
And loved your beauty with love false or true,
But one man loved the pilgrim soul in you,
And loved the sorrows of your changing face;

And bending down beside the glowing bars,
Murmur, a little sadly, how Love fled
And paced upon the mountains overhead
And hid his face amid a crowd of stars.

—*W. B. Yeats*

SNOW SHOWER WITH SUN

Right now I'm sipping coffee, thinking about you, how we once kissed on Church Street, how the cold, suddenly, disappeared as stars hovered in their glass coats then came in close to catch a glimpse because they know that first kisses stop time every time; and when I lift the cup to wake in the world where you are, I look up at this sky shining, turned on, blinding, a rush of pink and gold and white, a flowing hush ocean-sized where a young girl and her mother close their eyes and catch crystals on their tongues.

—Alexander Long

THE ABANDONED VALLEY

Can you understand being alone so long
you would go out in the middle of the night
and put a bucket into the well
so you could feel something down there
tug at the other end of the rope?

—Jack Gilbert

MIDWAY ATOLL

—after message from the Gyre, Chris Jordan

I flip through a stack of photographs, one more colorful than the next— the belly of each albatross chick a beautiful jumble: turquoise and yellow shards, the bright white of bottle caps, fluorescent magenta of someone's discarded toothbrush, peach of a tampon tube, royal blue lighter—nested within cages of shattered rib, twisted yards of knotted green string, shreds of translucent plastic sheeting, all so far from any land I've walked (2000 miles from the nearest continent out in the middle of the North Pacific), yet evidence in waste of my human presence; when I leave my children hungry for attention and drive myself to the ER a random Wednesday evening because I can't take a full breath for pains in my chest—I picture

this: blown open bodies, crevices of unexpected debris, feathers splayed
and matted, the elegant curve of bill, silent and still against pebbly sand
. . . and can't even say it to myself: *I was trying in my frenzy to feed you;*
please forgive me and remember my love.

—*Katrina Roberts*

WHERE YOU GO WHEN SHE SLEEPS

What is it when a woman sleeps, her head bright
In your lap, in your hands, her breath easy now as though it had
    never been
Anything else, and you know she is dreaming, her eyelids
Jerk, but she is not troubled, it is a dream
That does not include you, but you are not troubled either,
It is too good to hold her while she sleeps, her hair falling
Richly on your hands, shining like metal, a color
That when you think of it you cannot name, as though it has just
Come into existence, dragging you into the world in the wake
Of its creation, out of whatever vacuum you were in before,
And you are like the boy you heard of once who fell
Into a silo full of oats, the silo emptying from below, oats
At the top swirling in a gold whirlpool, a bright eddy of grain, the boy,
You imagine, leaning over the edge to see it, the noon sun breaking
Into the center of the circle he watches, hot on his back, burning
And he forgets his father's warning, stands on the edge, looks down,
The grain spinning, dizzy, and when he falls his arms go out, too thin
For wings, and he hears his father's cry somewhere, but is gone
Already, down in the gold sea, spun deep in the heart of the silo,
And when they find him, his mouth, his throat, his lungs
Full of the gold that took him, he lies still, not seeing the world
Through his body but through the deep rush of the grain
Where he has gone and can never come back, though they drag him
Out, his father's tears bright on both their faces, the farmhands
Standing by blank and amazed—you touch that unnamable
Color in her hair and you are gone into what is not fear or joy
But a whirling of sunlight and water and air full of shining dust

That takes you, a dream that is not of you but will let you
Into itself if you love enough, and will not, will never let you go.

—T. R. Hummer

THE THIEF

What is it when your man sits on the floor
in sweatpants, his latest project
set out in front of him like a small world, maps
and photographs, diagrams and plans, everything
he hopes to build, invent or create,
and you believe in him as you always have,
even after the failures, even more now
as you set your coffee down
and move toward him, to where he sits
oblivious of you, concentrating
in a square of sun—
you step over the rulers and the blue graph-paper
to squat behind him, and he barely notices,
though you're still in your robe
which falls open a little as you reach
around his chest, feel for the pink
wheel of each nipple, the slow beat
of his heart, your ear pressed to his back
to listen—and you are torn,
not wanting to interrupt his work
but unable to keep your fingers
from dipping into the ditch of his pants,
torn again with tenderness
for the way his flesh grows unwillingly
toward your curved palm, toward the light,
as if you had planted it, this sweet root,
your mouth already an echo of its shape—
you slip your tongue into his ear
and he hears you, calling him away
from his work, the angled lines of his thoughts,

into the shapeless place you are bound
to take him, over bridges of bone, beyond
borders of skin, climbing over him
into the world of the body, its labyrinth
of ladders and stairs—and you love him
like the first time you loved him,
with equal measures of expectancy
and fear and awe, taking him with you
into the soft geometry of flesh, the earth
before its sidewalks and cities,
its glistening spires,
stealing him back from the world he loves
into this other world he cannot build without you.

—*Dorianne Laux*

If there is any single emotion that identifies us as human, it is love. We succumb to romantic love, sexual love, the unconditional love of children. We fall in love with each other, but also with cities, with books, with seasons of the year. We have all been in love—elated, broken-hearted, chastened or ecstatically transfigured—and there is little in life that marks us so indelibly.

Consider a love affair—your first crush or some missed opportunity, the long journey of a marriage or a summer fling, a lost love or an undying love—and try to capture it in a single sentence. You may want to distill an entire, long relationship as Polly Bee does, or capture a relationship in a single moment as Alex Long does in "Snow Shower with Sun." Task yourself to write without recourse to the tropes of sentimentality or the easy excesses of popular song. Consider your love affair as you would a beautiful, mysterious object, and fit it into a sentence, like a ring slipped over a finger.

CHAPTER ELEVEN

Prayer, Supplication and Wonder

A t a fundamental, even primal level, every poem is a prayer; every poem reaches out from the poet to some ineffable other—to God, to the cosmos or to nature, or simply to whatever exists beyond our understanding or our ken. The earliest poems that have come down to us have their roots in the oral tradition. It shouldn't surprise us that these poems tend to be songs of love, or tales about gods, and hymns, prayers or supplications to deities. Whether we read the Vedas, the Bible or *The Iliad,* we are confronted again and again with men and women grappling with their relationship to the divine.

In his poem "Matthew 6: 9-13," Fred Dings echoes the syntax and rhythm of the "Our Father" to offer his own version of "This, then, is how you should pray." Dings offers a litany of "things" that he recognizes as precious jewels, and he invokes them as holy artifacts. David Axelrod meditates on the nature of life, death and rebirth in his poem, and renders a solemn but ecstatic prayer while contemplating compost, where "buried stems of Brussels sprouts form bundles of leaves like hands folded in prayer."

The mundane details of our lives often prove to be the most redolent of a world or a power beyond the one we inhabit. In the poems below, such simple things as stars, water, crickets or chimney smoke provoke sensations of awe, meditations on eschatology, and prayers of wonder and of gratitude.

REMEMBERING SAN REMO

After the end, they'll bring you
To someplace like this, columns of light propped through a west-facing door,
People standing about, echo of shoe-taps,
The gloom, like a grease-soaked rag, like a slipped skin
Left in a corner, puddle
In back of the votive stick stands, matter-of-factly—

Under the lisp and cold glow of the flames
Everything stares and moves closer, faces and blank hands,
October the 1st, 1975,
The banked candles the color of fresh bone,
Smoke rising from chimneys beyond the beyond,
Nightfires, your next address . . .

—Charles Wright

DRINKING CHAMPAGNE

When he first tasted sparkling wine, Dom Perignon
    imagined he was drinking stars,

bubbles like pearls, rising through liquid the thin
    color of beaten gold . . .

and now, overlooking the sea, the moon dribbling out
    its dabs of light, fingering

the silk trees' old thoughts, I feel it's as close as we are
    likely to come to celestial rewards,

though if I didn't know better in my bones, I'd still
    swear I would be the one

to get out of here alive, the one to forgive the stars
    for misleading us all this time.

—Christopher Buckley

SISTERS

Sisters, when they wrap up our parcels for the grave, we'll take off our aprons, break the looms, throw away the crochet, leave the kitchen sink, wash our hands clean, and ride the buggy to the moon.

—*Jie Tian*

METEOR SHOWERS, YOSEMITE

If, when a blind moth
eclipses the moon
outside of time
you can't see wishes
re-lit from the tail
ends of old wishes—
look up from a bed
of eyeless needles
to the owl's cry
vaporized into a streak
of light, a spark
stirred from the hot
bed of smoky stars,
little deaths you must
be ready for
with all your eyes.

—*Dixie Salazar*

BEHOLD—THIS COMPOST

Incipient emerald, nest of earthworms, July jungle in which children will race and squeal like the joyful creatures they were born to be—this is the garden I smothered in compost, and that I stood by all winter, kicking at its edges, loosening a clod, turning over a damp mat of leaves to listen to the many languages spoken in its café of perpetual heat, where steam of rot rises, where shoots of chestnuts are delicate as a musician's fingers, and buried stems of Brussels sprouts form bundles of leaves like hands folded in prayer, where rags of sod struggle like Jesus, reversing direction, sending up pale yellow and passionate hair, celebrating the light returned from the south this blustery April day I've waited for, when I take a stride into the garden and shovel down in the volcanic soil, turning it over again, turning under russet leaves and whirlybirds that, on the first warm day, sprouted ten thousand maple seedlings, and besides, what else is there to do with a life as imperfectable as ours, where all that's alive is somebody else's food and what was alive is the soil from which it grew?

—*David Axelrod*

DAYBREAK

It would be simple to believe
all this matters, that the sea
roars words in a final language,
that a stone contains an answer
to the wind's insistence, that you can
take what you need—stone, sand, sea,
the wind's wild words—and hug
the earth you were born to
and say nothing, like a guest
who arrives late to a great silence.

—*Philip Levine*

READING WANG WEI
AFTER MEETING WITH DR. WONG

I wait under rain-glazed clouds, a cup of Syrah
in hand atop Sierra Madre Canyon,
raising my gaze up as I watch the moon rise
behind the mountain, listening for crickets,
and impatient for the promises of spring, the sounds
of summer, I slowly sip the dregs of last year's

wine, full-bodied and pure as baby's breath—
where did my shooting star go?

—Carol Lem

MATTHEW 6: 9-13

Blue herons that fish in silence,
webs that sag with dew,
old pines in mist,
the snow at sea,
and hues as they merge in evening,
rain on mossed rocks,
and crackling flames,
and a breeze touched with brine,
and leaf-stained light in autumn,
Gandhi, Bach, Monet, Maria,
and a stream pool laved with pollen,
the surf as it lathers
and then hisses on the beaches,
the twilight, the stillness

                      :these things.

—Fred Dings

REDWING BLACKBIRDS

This morning they came like the dying
reclaiming their old lives, delirious
with joy right on the seam of spring,
streaming in by the tattered thousands
like black leaves blowing back onto the trees,
but the homeless know what's expected by now,
and when the farmer fired into their body,
they rose all around me like trembling

black wounds gaping red at the shoulders,
a river of pain draining into the sky:

tonight, as I look at the cold sky
and its flock of blue-white scars,
I can't yet turn from Orion's red star
whose trembling red light has traveled for years
to die now into any eyes that will hold it.

—*Fred Dings*

THE MIGRAINE'S ART

Blackwork—

this wanting to unravel, to travel lonely at the edge of the road

yoked to an undiscovered purpose, wintry

and so far gone

this me, this mist, this ashy unraveling chained

to the axe in my crown

harried by heaven's hurt

and craving a beggar's bed

for the fox is out and bells are tolling fire

or priests,

their knuckles a nick in my skull.

—*Deborah Bogen*

AUTUMN

Cathedral of my enchantments, autumn wind, I grew old giving thanks.

—Czesław Miłosz

Every poet can identify to some degree with the sentiment of the Sufi poet Rumi when he writes:

> You healed my wounded hunger and anger,
> and made me a poet who sings about joy.

When we "sing about joy" in our poems, we create a sublime music. Make a list of things for which you are thankful, and work that list into a poem of gratitude. Write a prayer—to God, to the void, or to the unseen powers that seem to guide us through life—and let that prayer manifest your joy at the things of the world. Take a single, specific object of delight, such as Fred Dings' blackbirds, or Christopher Buckley's champagne, and coax from your memory as many particular instances as you can in which that thing has moved you. Nothing you might choose—rain, morning light, pianos, autumn leaves—is too incidental or irrelevant. Invite wonder into your poems.

CHAPTER TWELVE

The Catalog Poem

One of the oldest modes of poetic composition is the catalog poem, which reaches back as far as Homer. In more modern times we have Walt Whitman, the great cataloger, and his poetic heir, Alan Ginsberg. We might construct our own catalog of poets who have enjoyed the fruits of this strategy of utilizing lists of concrete details and concrete nouns. The catalog poem counts on the poet's ability to marshal lists of the world's abundance while keeping the specifics fresh and engaging. In the catalog poem, less is not more—more is more.

Sometimes called a "List Poem," the catalog poem depends upon accretion and accrual, and there is a special emphasis on rhythm, specificity and resolution. The trick in writing a one-sentence catalog poem is to avoid monotony in rhythm and in syntax, and to come inductively to a conclusion, summary statement or resonant image that transforms the material. A poet must be keenly aware of sound value—assonance and consonance; polysyllabic versus monosyllabic word choices—and be attuned to rhythms that increase and decrease speed and intensity. Inventive quantification and original image-making also support the project of the catalog poem. A good catalog poem requires that the poet bring the observational skills of a detective to the project. A list of first-hand experiential details, concrete nouns and objects in a specific environment, helps poets avoid the grand abstractions that can make poems private and inaccessible. What can you build, with an unpredictable outcome, from the materials on hand?

THE CUP OF GARDENIAS

Bouganvillia—majenta, full regalia
Star Jasmine—green & white, carpeting the trellis
Damask roses—pale cream with open lips
Red Lion Amaryllis—assertion of trumpet power
A Shrimp Plant that hummingbirds love—ruffled pink and
    honeycombed brick
But on the Gardenia bush—though many buds fat as cherubs,
only two white blossoms unfurled,

so Marilyn cuts them
with her silver scissors
for me, and
in a cup translucent as dragonfly wings
in concept and texture,
they float
next to my head,
whirling in sleeper's flight:

a grail.

—*Diane Wakoski*

SELF-PITY'S CLOSET

Appetite without hunger, unquenchable
thirst, secret open wounds, long parades
of punishments, anger honed and glinting
in the sun, an empty bird call, the wind
driving a few leaves, the grass bent down,
shivering, running in place, far off a dog
barking and barking, the skin sticky, the crotch
itchy, the tongue stinging, words thrust from the mouth
like bottles off a bridge, tangy acids
of disgust, dank memory of backs, of eyebrows
raised, cool expressions after vast and painful

declarations, subtle humiliations creeping up
like the smell of wet upholstery, dial tone
in the brain, days swollen and matted
like newspaper melting in the bathtub,
the conviction your friends never really
loved you, the certitude you deserved
no better, never have, the faucet drilling
the sink, a bug bouncing against the window:
go away, make them all go away.

—*Michelle Boisseau*

NOSTALGIC CATALOGUE

for Gerald Stern

clumps of spinach gritty with sand in the seaside lot;
calabash tangle foaming in the surf,
shaking its bracelets of hollow beads and seafluff;
black urchins bubbling in the tinned bucket,
spikes, tentacles, needles, and dimpled shells,
poisonous bundles decipherable to the Chinese,
delicious to eat;
the Portuguese hiking their carnival skirts,
rolling the cuffs of their khaki pants
and wading the reef out to sea;
sour stars of green fruit in newspaper cones;
bad teeth, medicine in blue bottles, lip-paint;
78s heavy as stone hissing under the roosterheadof the phonograph;
soldiers on a cluttered bureau,
sepia-toned portraits splashed with fine lines of script;
Jeeps, artillery on trailers, troop carriersin a long caravan,
their headlights switched on, yellow through the afternoon;
Army surplus dumps, powdered cream in mud-colored tins;
Pilot crackers, canned meat, dried Chinese plum seeds brined in salt;
incense sticks in a sand bowl, brass temple bells,and black-lacquer
    Japanese trays;

an urn of ashes, a wooden doll
the old folks wept over odd days;
the sizzle of rain on the highway, on the sea,
on the far approach of night traffic on its way toward town;
lipstick Buicks with white interiors
stopping roadside on Saturdays full of tourists
in sunglasses, hats, Bermuda shorts,and polka-dot dresses;
conch shell souvenirs, huge and pink-lipped,
white price tags dangling like liprings;
"76" stations with their jars of green oil,
free pens and shirt pocket calendars slick as a dog's tongue;
sexy pinups, orange-fleshed and cartoonlike
on the back wall by the lube-rack;
orders from uncles and telephones full of questions,
strange voices demanding somebody to be home;
a baby elephant in harness, pulling a wagon full of blue seats,
eating Pall Malls by the pack
in the dirt lot by the sugar mill;
the green milt of the koi pond,
the rusting screen of the cat-net that covered it,
its face-powder lilies with orange-flame hearts
and green bed quilts of pie-pan leaves;
the swatches of color-wheel fish splashing in them,
extraordinary with Chinese names unpronounceable,
full of fortune and strange tales;
the Green Lady rocking in her aqueous cradle of weeds,
rising from the sea at night, persistent in dreams,
in warnings, in the made-up stories of cousins who lie;
creeks full of silver and black-barred fish
that loved shrimp balled on small, golden hooks;
chilly waters and the undulant stripes of mullet schooled near shore;
coral cuts, the animalcula building that reef in your blood;
a kite, box-like, assembled in air,
holding its place in a high wind,
the sketch of an astonished face
bobbing over the temple grounds and grey tile roofs,
as old men chant unknowable tunes
and hand over the red strings.

—*Garrett Hongo*

The signature mark of autumn has arrived at last with the rains: orange of pumpkin, orange persimmon, orange lichen on rocks and fallen logs; a copper moon hung low over the orchard; moist, ruddy limbs of the madrone, russet oak leaf, storm-peeled redwood, acorns emptied by squirrels and jays; and mushrooms, orange boletes, Witch's Butter sprouting on rotted oak, the Deadly Galerina, and of course, chanterelles, which we'll eat tonight with pasta, goat cheese, and wine.

—*Gary Young*

A YARD SALE IN MID-APRIL

A briefcase
where he stored grandfather's papers, an abacus,
then a fake gold clock with two bells on its head, and odd barbeque
for inside-the-house cooking, about the size of a three-layer-cake,
a pencil from Russia with a green tip for sketching, the sky is above
all this, not in a religious sense, it notes this delight I take on rare
occasions, then it continues its own miracles, it does not matter
that I am not seeing things, matter, space, future, spirit,
all this does not matter, I step into the kitchen, give the abacus
to my niece, tell my daughter about my cooking, wander outside
under the clouds.
    —*Juan Felipe Herrera*

ODE TO MY TÍO PEPE

for my mother's brother

Dark skinned from cleaning patios,
middle-aged with a full head of hair
that smells of Vitalis,
he sports a mustache he shaves down
to a fine eyelash with a Gillette razor,
having never been married
or moved out of his parents' house,

always keeping his bedroom door
locked to protect his collection
of wooden Indian figurines,
antique teapots, and porcelain roosters,
acquired on Saturday afternoon drives
in his 1965 Mercedes Benz,
cherry-bomb red with glitter
and woofers that boom "Pop that Coochie,"
into town to buy amateur artwork
at yard sales, or estate sales
where he picked up
an early twentieth-century sofa
which is now in the living room
with a "Do Not Sit" sign taped on,
which also applies to the birch coffee table
on which rests a stack of *Architectural Digest,*
a magazine he thumbs through
every now and then with his legs crossed,
sipping Taster's Choice from a tin cup,
before Sunday arrives as well as the nephews,
who have slid into their teens so quickly,
and to whom he never raises his voice
when they become dust devils of trouble
out in the back desert,
he having more class
in one manicured fingernail
than the entire lower Coachella Valley,
my tío Pepe, who has fresh wine-in-a-box
sitting on top of the dryer,
will pour us Chardonnay
from a spigot into clear plastic cups
that sparkle as they catch the light
coming through the window
as we raise our hands
to toast him, his Mercedes,
his second-hand furniture,
his movie-star mustache,

the wooden figurines
and everything else he keeps
behind closed doors.

—John Olivares Espinoza

One of the traditional tasks of the poet is to cherish and save experience, to polish and preserve the details of experience. In the catalog poem, the poet reveals our humanity through the details that surround us and compose our world. It is an ideal vehicle in service of this charge. Your list can be as quotidian and mundane as the one in Juan Felipe Herrera's "A Yard Sale in Mid-April," but notice how Herrera keeps his poem moving swiftly along by judicious use of comma splices, so that the ending arrives fresh and unexpected. Be sure to pay attention to his resolution, what that last gesture manages to say—almost out of the blue—about worldly possessions.

John Olivares Espinoza's poem reveals how recollection and nostalgia can preserve ordinary objects and make them shine in memory no matter how commonplace or mundane they may be. Notice how much can be accomplished even in a short catalog such as the one Diane Wakoski offers here; her deep knowledge and appreciation of flowers renders a delicate hymn that focuses and distills the blossoms' grace. Tap whatever particular knowledge you may possess about birds, or trees, or clouds, or enumerate the eccentric incidentals that might occupy your pocket, purse or kitchen drawer. A careful list of these will contains rich images and evocative language, and may well add up to an imagistic epiphany.

Or use Garrett Hongo's tour-de-force of a catalog poem, "Nostalgic Catalog," as a model for a poem constructed out of your past. While recalling his childhood environments and specific childhood events, Hongo is very careful to select the most interesting and emblematic details, those with the most unusual sound value and visual interest, to present the reader with the joy and exotic atmosphere he recalls from his youth. Draw a list from your own memories, and build a poetic memorial of your treasured recollections.

It is possible as well to write a very effective catalog poem centered more on emotion and imagination than on concrete detail such as Michelle Boisseau has done in "Self Pity's Closet." Notice that her poet's eye and sense of craft anchor every emotion or abstraction in solid, specific imagery: "dial tone / in the brain, days swollen and matted / like newspaper melting in the bathtub" are just two of many examples.

It is profitable to begin a catalog poem as a sort of journal assignment. Make a list of everything you remember from a time, a place or an experience, then go down your list and edit, tossing out whatever is clichéd or too predictable; remove any detail that does not contribute to your overall focus. Edit your list a second time, qualifying the nouns and the details, and develop complex images from the individual items, sensations or events. Finally, looking again at our models, decide if your catalog is best resolved by a fresh summary statement or by a resonant image that will expand the emotion or the vision of the poem.

CHAPTER THIRTEEN

Take It To the Limit

We started this book with succinct one- and two-line poems supported by fundamental syntax—subject, verb and object. In those first poems, thought and emotion were distilled, and the essential transformation and revelation of experience took place in short order, and fit within the discrete frame of a single sentence. We then saw examples of this initial strategy expanded with the elasticity of a single breath, as Alan Ginsberg described it long ago, stretched to include more imagery and detail, more comment, but still trim and logical within the framework of the sentence. We offered sonnets, longer poems that employed rhetorical devices, and poems that traversed a good portion of the page and more.

The logical conclusion of this project is to take it to the limit: to find a subject with sufficient engaging detail, and see how long you can make the string of a single sentence play out and still come to a successful and rewarding conclusion. With more material to marshal, you will need to be especially concerned with rhythm and with music as you keep your vision or narrative propelled forward. You may need to tap into some deep reservoir of psychic energy to drive the details and your poetic voice over a vast landscape; or you may want to work symphonically, with theme, variation and recapitulation. You will need all of your rhetorical moves, syntactical tricks and rule-breaking resourcefulness to carry a more substantial cargo that still works as a single unit—the sentence.

In his poem "Commuters," Edward Hirsch elaborates a subtle but terrifying image of drowning throughout his introspective meditation in the persona of a commuter. This image grows more and more powerful, until the poem and its narrator are overwhelmed by a hallucinatory sea. James Harms knows his territory well, and the penetrating details and precise images in his poem "So Long, Sunset Boulevard" spiral before us while supporting and elaborating an overarching theme of loss. Katrina Roberts shows us what can be done with a collection of scientific details. Her perfect control of syntax is coupled with a dramatic question inherent in her narrative, a vision quest to discover our humanity. We end with Bonnie Bolling's tour-de-force, "The C Word." To bring off a one-sentence poem of such impressive length, a poet must have command of grammatical and rhetorical skills, know when breaking the rules is effective and profitable, and he or she must have discovered an entirely credible voice of introspection. Every poem written in the first person is in some respect a persona poem, and there must be a credible interiority and psychological motivation to keep the poem moving successfully at this length.

Select any of these poems as a model, or choose something entirely of your own invention and see if you can take your sentence to the limit.

COMMUTERS

It's that vague feeling of panic
That sweeps over you
Stepping out of the # 7 train
At dusk, thinking, *This isn't me*
Crossing a platform with the other
Commuters in the worried half-light
Of evening, *that must be*

Someone else with a newspaper
Rolled tightly under his arm
Crossing the stiff, iron tracks
Behind the train, thinking, *This*
Can't be me stepping over the tracks
With the other commuters, slowly crossing
The parking lot at the deepest
Moment of the day, wishing

That I were someone else, wishing
I were anyone else but a man
Looking out at himself as if
From a great distance,
Turning the key in his car, starting
His car and swinging it out of the lot,

Watching himself grinding uphill
In a slow fog, climbing past the other
Cars parked on the side of the road,
The cars which seem ominously empty
And strange,
and suddenly thinking
With a new wave of nausea
This isn't me sitting in this car
Feeling as if I were about to drown
in the blue air, *that must be*
Someone else driving home to his
Wife and children on an ordinary day
Which ends, like other days,
With a man buckled into a steel box,
Steering himself home and trying
Not to panic

In the last moments of nightfall
When the trees and the red-brick houses
Seem to float under green water
And the streets fill up with sea lights.

—*Edward Hirsch*

ANTIQUES ROAD SHOW

On the advice of my urologist, I'm standing, instead of sitting, in front
of my workshop, asking about Jimi Hendrix, who's popped up in a
student poem, but no one has the first idea who he was, not one fuzzy
driving bump of bass, or drained, psychedelic high-note bubbles up from

the synaptic mudflats, firing a riff from "All Along the Watchtower" or "Foxy Lady," there's not one historical nanosecond of "Purple Haze" flashback to the '60s, and my god, even with music—the lingua franca of the young—I realize I'm all alone up here, and might as well bring up Bunny Berigan and "I Can't Get Started" as dear, early-departed Jimi, and when I read the line from the Veinberg poem in our text about roasting marshmallows with Taras Bulba on a beach in Carmel, I'm the only one busting a gut, and it's still a half hour to the break, when I can get down the hall to the Mens room, where I find myself thinking about the Trent River, that old bloke fishing off the banks who came across a rubbish pile with half a dozen paintings he hauled off to the British version of Antiques Road Show, one watercolor of Columbus landing in Hispañiola, and another of local Cubans in costume, on which the expert used his pointer to trace the clear signature of Winslow Homer, which a number of folks must have seen and walked away from asking, "Who's he when he's home?" leaving this enterprising geezer to be told it's worth 30,000 pounds—100,000 if it were in better nick—and unlike all those on the show who swear they'll keep it in the family and never sell, he says he's putting it on the block tomorrow and giving the money to his daughter for school—no point in keeping it around and letting it grow duller, collecting dust, like the rest of us.

—Christopher Buckley

SO LONG, SUNSET BOULEVARD

Red Foxx (is he still alive?) and I shared
a friend who ended up
as strung out as a pair of boxers
on a nice day in West Virginia, the traffic
along Route 50 lifting just enough breeze
to air out the underwear,
who started as a dealer and paid his mother's
rent and kept his brother
in private schools until he was old enough
to know enough

then ducked into the leaves and never said so long
to anyone, not to his best friend who ended up
I wish I knew, he was my friend, too,
not to Hollywood and the easy marks, all those
tourists to Junkieland ready for
anything wrapped in foil, not to Highland
and Las Palmas and Wilcox and Vine,
all the cross streets west of Gower,
not to here and here's the rub:
he never said so long to Sunset Boulevard,
which has a way of seeming endless as it winds
toward the Pacific, where anyone
can end up out of road and alone
in the crowd above the sea, where
anyone can stand on the bluffs and watch
the ironic sunset, the air alive
with ozone, with all
the parts per million, the grenadine pink
and safety vest orange, where Red Foxx
if he's still alive sips coffee
at a picnic table near
the phone booths, our friend
waiting, his hand
on a receiver and thinking about
what's next: a meeting with
his brother's teacher, a date with his
mother's gutters (all that clutter and sag),
but for now the waiting around for
a sound at sunset, the wind
in a dropped bottle, the sizzle
of waves drawing back, a bell above
the traffic, a chance to say
Hey and how much, to say OK and so long.

—*James Harms*

CHINCHORRO

In the Archaeology Museum of San Miguel de Azapa at the University of Tarapacá in Chile an entire family lies wrapped in sheets of muslin as though sleeping—yet each inhaled last sometime circa 5000 BC: see, here's a newborn, here's a woman (their mother?) flanked by two children, here's a man, maybe a father, and a fetus; I see now I should perhaps have begun elsewhere: we set him free, the brother who did not come to live on this side, and all day, others down the beige hall left indentations and tossed white sheets, to move past doors pushed without intention ajar so one might overhear or glimpse pure joy, taking their small loaves bunted pink or blue out into human air for the first time, while canned songs of lilting *"noels"* seeped from unseen speakers to make my eyes stream with self-pity and hatred for the happy ones who carried bouquets of raucous red and pink roses, strident lilies, toward their cars, juggling carriers and blankets, bottles and cards, while I—did I mention hatred?—clamped the pale mint consolation prize against my deflated belly, the satin box in which evidence of your birdy existence hid: footprints though you never walked, two hats though your head would never bob in song, a tiny cotton shirt like a straightjacket to tie across your heart had it been beating, its sleeve-ends stitched shut so your nails couldn't scratch your milky cheeks; and there *I* was—I could have been anyone—all my lovely soft organs removed, my brain and marrow tapped, my thin skin peeled back to reveal every ugly bit of what was left of me, my hollowed arms reinforced with sticks to wrap mummy-tight around heaving shoulder, my face still wet—and which would, forever after when at last I'd dried out, require new features of white ash paste, a mask of sea lion skin, and a thick coat of manganese paint in black.

—*Katrina Roberts*

THE 'C' WORD

It was the '60s and there was still that war and I was five—maybe six and there were eight of us plus a cousin and a Labrador Retriever flying along in the red Mercury station wagon, me and my family, because that's the only flying we ever did, on the way to Florida or maybe to Yellowstone, or the time we went to Mount Rushmore to see those faces carved, oddly enough, into the mountainside, just after the Perkins twins were drafted, and later only the one coming back, but no matter the destination there all of us were inside the red Mercury station wagon, stopping at roadside motels with neon signs, leopard print bedspreads and empty swimming pools and there I was in the way-back seat that faced backward because I was the fifth child of six and a girl to boot, and fortunate not to have been 'put down' in the backyard creek with the surplus kittens that one summer in Michigan and so there I sat in the back on the red vinyl upholstery which was torn in places from the dog's dew claws and my dad had patched the holes with something like red duct tape which had melted in the hot car and the summer heat because this is before someone invented air conditioning or figured out how to blast coolness into the car without poisoning everyone and the glue on the tape melted just enough so that your butt and thighs stuck to the glue and also to the seat, and me in a little hand-me-down skirt with my hand-me-down cotton underpants that were baggy because the elastic had stretched out or broken apart entirely around the legs and that tiny piece of cloth that served as a covering for my crotch stuck to the melting glue from the red duct tape and tore away because it was August and extremely hot in the car and one of my cousins notices this problem I am having with my lingerie and begins hooting with laughter and pointing because my crotch, now fully exposed, is also stuck to the glue on the seat and I had never realized before then that crotches—more importantly *my* crotch— had so many small parts hidden inside the folds of it or that it might in some way prove amusing to my cousin or anyone else for that matter because it was just one of those body parts that you couldn't see very well like your butt or something behind you though I knew about the small hole where the pee comes out—called a 'pee hole' and of course the one on your butt for pooh called a 'butt hole'—all very sensible names, but there it was, my *clitoris,* exposed to all for what had to be the first time because I had never noticed it before but right away there was the sort of crazy appalling embarrassment that you feel when you know something has happened because of everyone staring and reacting or looking away even in their own private embarrassments, but you are not exactly sure what because such a thing has not yet been part of your experience but there I was with my clitoris stuck fast to the seat and I have always thought since that day the word 'clitoris' or 'clit' for short is the kind of word that embarrasses everyone except for my doctor, who is a woman by the way, but my other doctor from before was a man and it was not easy to talk to him about certain body parts, the clitoris being one of them, I mean think about a kindly old gray-haired gentleman who isn't someone you might generally think to talk to about your clitoris so you refuse to mention it or you substitute abstract language for it such as 'you know, that one little *thing* down there' or you point in a disinterested fashion to your lower extremities as though such a thing doesn't really matter at all, that you just *wondered* is all and thought you should come in and *inquire* about some such when the truth is that it is *killing* you somehow because some creepy older boy the other night at that disgusting toga party did something unspeakably weird to it with his fingers or teeth or maybe some hand-held device you've never seen before and you don't really remember because of all the drinking and smoking beforehand and you are still trying to understand why you even agreed to hook-up with some creepy older boy and you just hope and pray that this kindly old— but old in a good, non-creepy-doctor-guy way *notices* that *something* is not quite right so you try pointing in the direction of the most painful part although the entire thing is so small, and although he is intently peering at your clitoris through some sort of magnifying glass you can't believe he doesn't notice because you yourself have checked it with a mirror and you are absolutely certain that something down there is terribly wrong, something is swollen on one side and hurts terribly every time you take a step but you can't bring yourself to *touch* it in front of him or even to say the word, can't say 'clitoris' because you actually aren't even sure how to pronounce it because no one ever said this forbidden word at your house except your cousin and he is a terrible speller and speaker of language in general and has actually spent some time in prison though you can't say if his refusal to accept the fact that he has serious sexual issues, and his protesting of that fact by way of breaking the law— not to mention his fleeing to Canada—had anything to do with your clitoris being glued to the backseat of the station wagon that terribly hot August, but how doubly embarrassing to mispronounce the word when your doctor is staring right at it, so you wonder if it is 'clitoris' with the accent on the first syllable or 'clitoris' with the accent on the second syllable and there is also the embarrassment about its actual function and main purpose for taking up space on your body down there, the fact that it has only one purpose really and it would just be so much easier all around if it were located, say, near your elbow though it might be too easily bumped if it were there, and can you just imagine your heart-felt obsession to bump into people, how you might fall in love with strangers even, if your clitoris were on your elbow—how awkward it would be to slow dance in junior high or stand close to strangers in line at the post office or if you stumbled so your son or your professor or your best friend's husband or President Obama had to grab your elbow to keep you from falling—if only it were on your hip or the top of your foot or behind your ear because it is always so much trouble for anyone to get to it and there would not be such lingering remorse if you were to hook-up with a creep if you never even had to get naked, and of course the only way to see your own clitoris is to be panty-less and holding a mirror and if you have ever walked in on someone panty-less and holding a mirror or even worse if someone has walked in on *you* while you are panty-less and holding a mirror than you know what I mean about embarrassment but one's own clitoris can't be seen by looking down from ones own viewpoint above because it is very different then the penis, which points all over the place for the entire world to see and you can hold a penis in your hand and it actually has some weight to it and I knew a lot more about penises before I even knew the existence of clitorises or that I might actually *have* one, but oh no, the clitoris hides from the world and the actual word is a mouthful to say what with the hard 'c' sound and then the 't' sound in the middle and that hissing 's' at the end but even so no one ever calls you a 'clit' or a 'clitoris' in the way they might call you a 'dick' or a 'cunt' because for some reason 'clit' is not a bad word with a bad connotation (but even so just try yelling it out at a party or in the bus station or in line at the grocery store) but no, actually its connotation is one that brings to mind some sort of pleasure yet in an embarrassing way, which is why you were beside yourself with unfathomable, unimaginable horror in the back of the red Mercury station wagon that hot day, with your cousin who was pointing and sneering because your clitoris had stuck fast to the melting duct tape on the seat, so you did the only thing you could, the only thing you knew to do—you peeled your poor clitoris off the seat and spent some time rubbing it, trying to make everything feel better.

DAVID AXELROD'S most recent collection of poems, *The Cartographer's Melancholy,* won the Spokane Prize and was a finalist for the Oregon Book Award. His new collection, *What Next, Old Knife?,* is forthcoming from Lost Horse Press in February 2012. He is editor of *basalt: a journal of fine & literary arts.*

POLLY BEE lives and writes in Ojai, California. Her book is *Scattershot,* from Bosie Books.

WILLIAM BLAKE was an English poet, painter and printmaker. Blake is now considered a seminal figure in the history of both the poetry and visual arts of the Romantic Age.

ROBERT BLY has been recognized as a seminal and important force in American poetry and poetry in translation for decades. His recent books are *Eating the Honey of Words: New & Selected Poems* and *Talking into the Ear of a Donkey.*

DEBORAH BOGEN lives in Pittsburg. Her books include *Landscape with Silos,* winner of the 2005 X. J. Kennedy Poetry Prize, and *Let Me Open You a Swan,* winner of the 2009 Elixir Press Antivenom Poetry Prize.

MICHELLE BOISSEAU was awarded a 2010 NEA fellowship. Her fourth book of poems, *A Sunday in God-Years,* was published in 2009 by University of Arkansas Press, which also published her third book, *Trembling Air,* a PEN USA finalist, 2003. Her textbook, *Writing Poems* (Longman), is in its 8th edition. She is professor of English at the University of Missouri-Kansas City.

BONNIE BOLLING is a poet who lives in Long Beach, California, and Bahrain. Her collection of poems *In the Kingdom of the Sons* was chosen by Tom Sleigh to win the 2011 Liam Rector Poetry Prize.

JAN BOTTIGLIERI lives and writes in Schaumburg, Illinois, and has been an associate editor for RHINO since 2004. Bottiglieri's poems have appeared in *Margie, Court Green, After Hours, Diagram, Bellevue Literary Review, Pearl, Apercus Quarterly* and in the anthologies *Illinois Writers: Where We Live, Brute Neighbors,* and *Solace in So Many Words.*

BRIAN BRODEUR is the author of *Natural Causes* (2012), which won the 2011 Autumn House Poetry Prize; *Other Latitudes* (2008), winner of the University of Akron Press's 2007 Akron Poetry Prize; and *So the Night Cannot Go on without Us* (2007), which won the Fall 2006 White Eagle Coffee Store Press Poetry Chapbook Award. He is editor/publisher of the blog, "How A Poem Happens."

SHARON BRYAN is the author of *Salt Air* (1983), *Objects of Affection* (1987), *Flying Blind* (1996) and *Sharp Stars* (2009), which won the Isabella Stewart Gardner Poetry Award. Bryan's work as an editor includes *Where We Stand: Women Poets on the Literary Tradition* (1994) and *Planet on the Table: Poets on the Reading Life* (2003), which she co-edited with William Olsen.

CHRISTOPHER BUCKLEY'S eighteenth book of poetry, *White Shirt,* was published by the University of Tampa Press in 2011. With Gary Young he has edited the anthologies *Bear Flag Republic: Prose Poems and Poetics from California* and *The Geography of Home: California's Poetry of Place.* Most recently with Christopher Howell, he has edited *Aspects of Robinson: Homage to Weldon Kees.*

SUZANNE BUFFAM is the author of two collections of poetry, *Past Imperfect* (House of Anansi), which won the Gerald Lampert Award for the best first book of poetry published in Canada in 2005, and *The Irrationalist,* published in 2010 by Canarium Books in the United States, and House of Anansi in Canada.

ROBERT CREELEY first received fame in 1962 from his poetry collection *For Love.* He later won the Bollingen Prize, among many others, and held the position of New York Poet Laureate from 1989 until 1991. He was elected a Fellow of the American Academy of Arts and Sciences in 2003. His *Selected Poems, 1945-2005,* edited by Benjamin Friedlander, was published by University of California Press, 2008.

BRAD CRENSHAW is the author of *My Gargantuan Desire,* published by Greenhouse Review Press in 2010. He has also published a chapbook, *Limits of Resurrection,* and a new chapbook, *Propagandas,* is forthcoming from Kattywompus Press.

e.e. cummings was an American poet, painter, essayist, author and playwright. He wrote close to 3,000 poems, two autobiographical novels, four plays and several essays, and his work includes numerous drawings and paintings.

J.V. CUNNINGHAM was a poet, critic and teacher who wrote spare, finely wrought verse. His epigrammatic poems draw on his talent as a poet, and upon his celebrated translations of Martial and other Latin poets. His work can be found in *The Poems of J. V. Cunningham,* Sparrow Press/Ohio University Press, 1996.

KATE DANIELS' first book of poetry, *The White Wave* (Pittsburgh, 1984), won the Agnes Lynch Starrett Poetry Prize. *The Niobe Poems* (Pittsburgh, 1988) received honorable mention for the Paterson Poetry Prize. *Four Testimonies* was selected by Dave Smith for his imprint *Southern Messenger Series,* and published by LSU Press in 1998. A fourth volume, *A Walk in Victoria's Secret,* was published in 2010 in the same series. She was recently named the winner of the 2011 Hanes Award for Poetry by the Fellowship of Southern Writers.

FRED DINGS is the author of two books of poetry, *After the Solstice* and *Eulogy for a Private Man.* He currently teaches at the University of South Carolina.

JENNIFER KWAN DOBBS' first collection, *Paper Pavilion* (White Pine Press 2007), received the White Pine Press Poetry Prize and the Sheila Motton Book Award, and her chapbook, *Song of a Mirror,* was a finalist for the Tupelo Press Snowbound Series Chapbook Award.

JOHN DONNE, English poet, satirist, lawyer and priest, is the pre-eminent representative of the metaphysical poets. His poems are known for their strong, sensual style and include sonnets, love poetry, religious poems, Latin translations, epigrams, elegies, songs, satires and sermons.

JOHN OLIVARES ESPINOZA'S most recent poetry collection is *The Date Fruit Elegies* (Bilingual Review Press, 2008). His recent work appears in *The American Poetry Review* and ZYZZYVA.

ROBERT FROST'S poems are perhaps the most beloved of any American poet of the twentieth century. His first two books, *A Boy's Will* and *North of Boston,* established his reputation, which grew with each succeeding book. He famously recited a poem at the inauguration of President John F. Kennedy, and his poems in traditional verse forms have a permanent place in the poetic landscape of America.

JACK GILBERT has been a major voice in American poetry for the last fifty years. His first book, *Views of Jeopardy,* won the 1962 Yale Series of Younger Poets Competition. A Guggenheim Fellowship, Lannan Literary Award for Poetry, NEA Fellowship, and two National Book Critics Circle Awards are among his most notable awards. *The Dance Most of All* is his most recent book.

MICHAEL HANNON is the author of several books of poetry including *Poems & Days, Ordinary Messengers* and *Trusting Oblivion.* He has also published many limited editions of his poems, and has collaborated with several fine printers, and with the artist William T. Wiley.

C. G. HANZLICEK is the author of seven books of poetry: *Living in It, Stars* (winner of the 1977 Devins Award for Poetry), *Calling the Dead, A Dozen for Leah, When There Are No Secrets, Mahler: Poems and Etchings* and *Against Dreaming.* He has translated Native American songs, *A Bird's Companion,* and poems from the Czech, *Mirroring: Selected Poems of Vladimir Holan,* which won the Robert Payne Award from the Columbia University Translation Center in 1985. He recently retired from teaching at California State University, Fresno, where he was the director of the Creative Writing Program.

JAMES HARMS is the author of eight books of poetry including two forthcoming volumes, *What to Borrow, What to Steal* (Marick Press, 2011) and *Comet Scar* (Carnegie Mellon University Press, 2012). He directs the low-residency MFA Program in Poetry at New England College, and is Professor of English at West Virginia University.

JUAN FELIPE HERRERA'S publications include fourteen collections of poetry, prose, short stories, young adult novels and picture books for children with twenty-one books in total in the last decade. Herrera was awarded the 2008 National Book Critics Circle Award in Poetry for *Half the World in Light.*

LEE HERRICK is the author of *This Many Miles from Desire* (WordTech Editions, 2007) and *Gardening Secrets of the Dead* (WordTech Editions, 2013). He lives in Fresno, California and teaches at Fresno City College and at the Sierra Nevada College low-residency MFA Program.

EDWARD HIRSCH has published eight books of poems, including *The Living Fire: New and Selected Poems* (2010), and four books of prose, among them *How to Read a Poem and Fall in Love with Poetry* (1999), a national bestseller.

JANE HIRSHFIELD has worked as a freelance writer, editor and translator, and her seven books of poetry have received numerous awards. *Given Sugar, Given Salt* was a finalist for the National Book Critics Circle Award, and her sixth collection, *After*, was shortlisted for the T.S. Eliot Prize (UK) and named a "Best Book of 2006" by *The Washington Post, The San Francisco Chronicle* and *The Financial Times.* She has written a book of essays, *Nine Gates: Entering the Mind of Poetry.*

JOHN HODGEN is the author of *Bread Without Sorrow*, winner of the Balcones Poetry Prize; *Grace*, winner of the Donald Hall Poetry Prize from AWP; and *Heaven & Earth Holding Company.* He is recipient of many other awards for his work, including the Foley Poetry Prize, the Ruth Stone Poetry Prize, the Grolier Prize, an Arvon Foundation Award, and the Chad Walsh Prize for Poetry. He teaches at Assumption College in Worcester, Massachusetts.

GARRETT HONGO is Distinguished Professor of Arts & Sciences at the University of Oregon. His most recent book of poetry is *Coral Road*, Knopf, 2011. He is the editor of *Open Boat: Poems from Asian America* (Anchor) and *Under Western Eyes: Personal Essays from Asian America* (Anchor).

CHRISTOPHER HOWELL'S tenth collection of poems, *Gaze*, was just released by Milkweed Editions. He lives in Spokane and teaches at Eastern Washington University's Inland NW Center for Writers.

T.R. HUMMER is the author of twelve books of poetry and prose, including *The Infinity Sessions* (LSU, 2005) and *The Muse in the Machine: Essays on Poetry and the Anatomy of the Body Politic* (University of Georgia Press, 2006). Formerly Editor in Chief of *Quarterly West, The Kenyon Review, New England Review* and *The Georgia Review*, he is professor of Creative Writing/English at Arizona State University.

MARK JARMAN is Centennial Professor at Vanderbilt University where he directs the MFA Program. *Bone Fires: New & Selected Poems* has been published by Sarabande Books.

JOHN KEATS was an English Romantic poet and one of the key figures in the second generation of the Romantic movement, despite the fact that his work had been in publication for only four years before his death. By the end of the 19th century he had become one of the most beloved of all English poets.

STEPHEN KESSLER is a poet, translator, essayist, editor and novelist. He is the author of eight books and chapbooks of original poetry, most recently *Burning Daylight;* fourteen books of literary translation, most recently *Desolation of the Chimera* by Luis Cernuda, winner of the 2010 Harold Morton Landon Translation Award from the Academy of American Poets; a novel, *The Mental Traveler;* and the essay collections *Moving Targets: On Poets, Poetry & Translation* and *The Tolstoy of the Zulus: On Culture, Arts & Letters.*

CHRISTINE KITANO grew up in Santa Monica and Los Angeles. Her first book is *Birds of Paradise* from Lynx House Press.

BILL KNOTT has been a unique and powerful presence in American poetry since the publication of his first book, *The Naomi Poems, Book One: Corpse and Beans* under the pseudonym Saint Geraud. Other books include *Becos* (1983), *Outremer*, winner of the Iowa Poetry Prize (1988), *Laugh at the End of the World: Collected Comic Poems 1969–1999* (2000), *The Unsubscriber* (2004), and *Stigmata Errata Etcetera* (2007), a collaboration with collages by the artist Star Black.

CAROL LEM'S most recent book is *Gathering the Pieces* (Greenhouse Review Press, 2010). She is the author of *Searchings, Grassroots, Don't Ask Why, The Hermit, The Hermit's Journey: Tarot Poems for Meditation, Moe* (Remembrance), and *The Shadow of the Plum*. A reading of selected poems from her current book, *Shadow of the Plum*, may be heard on her CD, *Shadow of the Bamboo*, with music by Masakazu Yoshizawa.

PHILIP LEVINE'S most recent book is *News of the World* from Knopf. He was Poet Laureate of the United States for 2011-2012, and has received the Pulitzer Prize and two National Book Awards for poetry, among his many honors.

LARRY LEVIS was one of the most original and important voices of twentieth century poetry. He suffered an untimely death at age 49. *The Selected Levis* is available from the University of Pittsburgh Press.

ALEXANDER LONG'S third book of poems, *Still Life,* won the 2011 White Pine Press Poetry Prize, and a chapbook of the same name won the 2010 Center for Book Arts Chapbook Competition. His other two collections are *Vigil* (2006) and *Light Here, Light There* (C & R Press, 2009). With Christopher Buckley, he is co-editor of *A Condition of the Spirit: The Life Work of Larry Levis* (Eastern Washington University Press, 2004). Long is an assistant professor of English at John Jay College, CUNY.

PERIE LONGO is Poet Laureate Emerita of Santa Barbara with three published books of poetry, the last being *With Nothing Behind but Sky: A Journey through Grief.* She has been on the staff of the Santa Barbara Writers Conference and led poetry workshops there for many years.

SUZANNE LUMMIS is an award-winning teacher at UCLA Extension where, since 1991, she has led the beginning through master class workshops in poetry. Lummis is principal editor of *Grand Passion: The Poetry of Los Angeles and Beyond* (LAPF). Her poetry collections include *Idiosyncrasie* (Illuminati) and *In Danger* (Heyday Books/Roundhouse Press) and one chapbook, *Falling Short of Heaven* (Pennywhistle).

DORIANNE LAUX'S most recent books are *Facts about the Moon* and *The Book of Men,* both from W. W. Norton, as well as *The Book of Women,* a chapbook from Red Dragonfly Press. She teaches poetry at North Carolina State University.

ANTONIO MACHADO was a Spanish poet, one of the leading members of the generation of '98, and one of the important voices of twentieth century poetry. The selection here is from his *Proverbios y Cantares*.

DEREK MCKOWN has taught creative writing at colleges and universities in California and New York. Greenhouse Review Press published his book of poetry, *Arrows in Hand,* in 2008. He currently lives in Lubbock, Texas where he is completing a Ph.D. in English.

JOSEPH MILLAR'S most recent book is *Blue Rust,* just out from Carnegie Mellon. He teaches in Pacific University's low residency MFA Program.

CZESŁAW MIŁOSZ received the Nobel Prize in Literature in 1980. His last books of poems are *New & Collected Poems (1931-2001)* and *Second Space: New Poems* (2004).

MARSHA DE LA O'S book of poetry, *Black Hope,* won the New Issues Press Poetry Prize and a Small Press Editor's Choice Award. She is the winner of the LA Poetry Award and the Ventura Poetry Festival Contest. With Phil Taggart, she is co-editor and publisher of the literary journal, *Askew.*

LINDA PASTAN has published a dozen books of poetry, and her awards include the Dylan Thomas Award, the Alice Fay di Castagnola Award from the Poetry Society of America, the Bess Hokin Prize *(Poetry Magazine),* the 1986 Maurice English Poetry Award (for *A Fraction of Darkness),* the Charity Randall Citation of the International Poetry Forum, and the 2003 Ruth Lilly Poetry Prize.

KENNETH REXROTH was an American poet, translator and critical essayist. He is regarded as a central figure in the San Francisco Renaissance, and paved the groundwork for that movement. His *Complete Poems* was published in 2003 by Copper Canyon Press.

JAMES RICHARDSON is Professor of English and Creative Writing at Princeton University. He has published several collections of poetry, criticism and aphorisms, including *Interglacial: New and Selected Poems* and *Aphorisms* (Ausable Press, 2004).

KATRINA ROBERTS is the author of several highly acclaimed books of poetry including *How Late Desire Looks,* which won the Peregrine Smith Poetry Prize; *The Quick; Friendly Fire,* winner of the Idaho Prize for Poetry; and most recently *Underdog* (University of Washington Press, 2011).

KAY RYAN has published seven volumes of poetry and was the sixteenth United States Poet Laureate, from 2008 to 2010. She was named a 2011 MacArthur Fellow. Her book *The Best of It: New and Selected Poems* was awarded the Pulitzer Prize.

DIXIE SALAZAR has published four books of poetry: *Hotel Fresno, Reincarnation of the Commonplace, Blood Mysteries* and *Flamenco Hips and Red Mud Feet* from University of Arizona Press in 2010. She has a novel, *Limbo,* from White Pine Press, and is also a visual artist, working primarily in oils. *Altar for Escaped Voices* will be published in The Ash Tree Poetry Series from Tebot Bach in 2012.

LUIS OMAR SALINAS was one of the leading Chicano poets as well as an important voice in contemporary American poetry for over thirty years. His first book, *Crazy Gypsy,* 1970, is now a classic of contemporary and Chicano poetry. He co-edited *Speaking for Ourselves* and *From the Barrio* in the late '60s and early '70s. He went on to publish eight books, and to receive many awards. His last book was *Elegy for Desire,* 2005, from the University of Arizona Press. *A New Selected Poems/Salinas Reader* is under preparation in The Ash Tree Poetry Series from Tebot Bach Press.

SHEILA SANDERSON is a rural Kentucky native who now lives in the high desert mountains of Arizona and teaches at Prescott College. Her work has appeared in *Alaska Quarterly Review, Cimarron Review, Crazyhorse* and *Southern Poetry Review.* Her book of poems is *Keeping Even,* Stephen F. Austin State University Press, 2011. "It So Happens" was originally published in *Cimarron Review,* Issue 144, Summer 2003.

WILLIAM SHAKESPEARE is widely considered the single greatest poet in English. This one-sentence sonnet is #66 in the Bard's sequence of 154 sonnets.

TIMOTHY SHEEHAN is the author of two books, *Yes,* and *Here,* both from Greenhouse Review Press.

GARY SOTO is the author of thirty-five books. His forthcoming book of poetry is *Sudden Loss of Dignity,* Tupelo Press, 2013. The Gary Soto Literary Museum is located at Fresno City College. He lives in Berkeley, California.

LISA M. STEINMAN, Kenan Professor of English & Humanities at Reed College, is the author of four volumes of poetry, *Lost Poems* (Ithaca House, 1976), *All That Comes to Light* (Arrowood Press, 1989), *A Book of Other Days* (Arrowood Press, 1993) and *Carslaw's Sequences* (University of Tampa Press, 2003). Her work has received recognition from the National Endowment for the Arts, the National Endowment for the Humanities, and the Rockefeller Foundation, among others. She co-edits the poetry magazine, *Hubbub.*

GERALD STERN'S *Lucky Life* won the 1977 Lamont Poetry Selection and established him as a major American poet. He has received many prestigious awards for his poetry, including the 1996 Ruth Lilly Poetry Prize and a National Book Award for poetry in 1998 for *This Time: New and Selected Poems.* He was Poet Laureate of New Jersey from 2000 to 2002, and received the Wallace Stevens Award from the Academy of American Poets in 2005. Since 2006, Stern has been a Chancellor of the Academy of American Poets.

JOSEPH STROUD has published five collections of poetry, most recently *Of This World: New and Selected Poems,* Copper Canyon Press, 2008. He was selected for a Witter Bynner Fellowship in poetry from the Library of Congress. He divides his time between his home in Santa Cruz, California, and a cabin in the Sierra Nevada.

COLE SWENSON'S most recent books are *Ours: poems on the gardens of Andre Le Notre,* University of California Press, 2008; *The Glass Age,* Alice James Books, 2007; *The Book of a Hundred Hands,* University of Iowa Press, Iowa City, 2005; *Goest,* Alice James Books, 2004; *Such Rich Hour,* 2001; *Oh,* 2000; and *Try,* 1999, which won the Iowa Poetry Prize.

JIE TIAN lives in Southern California and holds an MFA in Poetry from the University of California, Riverside. Her poems have appeared in *Pearl, Cloudbank, Phantom Seed, Squaw Valley Review, Sentence: A Journal of Prose Poetics,* and other publications.

RHETT ISEMAN TRULL'S first book, *The Real Warnings,* Anhinga Press, 2009, won the Brockman-Campbell Award, Devil's Kitchen Reading Award, and Oscar Arnold

Young Award. Her poetry has appeared in *The American Poetry Review, Prairie Schooner, The Southern Review,* and other publications. She is the editor of *Cave Wall.*

AMY UYEMATSU has published three poetry books: *Nights of Fire, Nights of Rain, 30 Miles from J-town,* and *Stone Bow Prayer,* Copper Canyon Press, 2005.

JON VEINBERG is the author of *An Owl's Landscape, Stickball Till Dawn, Oarless Boats, Vacant Lots* and most recently, *The Speed Limit of Clouds.* With Ernesto Trejo he was editor of *Piecework: 19 Fresno Poets.*

DIANE WAKOSKI began her poetry career in New York City from 1960-73. Since 1975 she has been Poet-in-Residence at Michigan State University. She has published more than twenty collections of poetry, most recently *The Diamond Dog,* Anhinga Press, 2010.

LAUREN WATEL is a fiction writer and poet who lives with her son in Decatur, Georgia.

WALT WHITMAN, poet, essayist and journalist, was a part of the transition between transcendentalism and realism, incorporating both views in his works. Whitman is among the most influential of American poets, and is often called the father of free verse. He is famous primarily for his poetry collection *Leaves of Grass.*

WILLIAM CARLOS WILLIAMS' major collections are *Spring and All* (1923), *Pictures from Brueghel and Other Poems* (1962), and *Paterson* (1963). Early in his career he was involved with the Imagist movement but had rejected it by the time *Spring and All* was published in 1923. Williams is more strongly associated with the American Modernist movement, and he sought to renew language through the fresh, raw language that grew out of America's cultural and social idiom.

PAUL WILLIS is a professor of English at Westmont College and the current Poet Laureate of Santa Barbara, California. His most recent books of poetry are *Rising from the Dead,* WordFarm, 2009, and *Visiting Home,* Pecan Grove Press, 2008.

DONALD WOLFF teaches at Eastern Oregon University. His first poetry collection, *Soon Enough,* was published by Wordcraft in 2007. He is now completing his second collection, *What's Close to Me.*

CHARLES WRIGHT, winner of the Pulitzer Prize, the National Book Critics Circle Award, the National Book Award, and the Griffin Poetry Prize, is recently retired from the University of Virginia. His most recent book is *Outtakes,* Sarabande Books, 2010.

WILLIAM BUTLER YEATS was an Irish poet and playwright, and one of the foremost figures of twentieth century literature. In 1923 he was awarded the Nobel Prize in Literature as the first Irishman so honored. Major works, including *The Tower* (1928) and *The Winding Stair and Other Poems* (1929) were written after he received the Nobel Prize.

DAVID YOUNG is the author of eleven books of poetry, most recently *Field of Light and Shadow: Selected and New Poems,* Knopf, 2010, in which "Ohio" appears. He taught for many years at Oberlin College and is still active as editor of FIELD and of books from Oberlin College Press.

GARY YOUNG is the author of seven books of poetry including *No Other Life,* which won the William Carlos Williams Award. His most recent book is *Even So: New and Selected Poems.* With Christopher Buckley he has edited the anthologies *Bear Flag Republic: Prose Poems and Poetics from California* and *The Geography of Home: California's Poetry of Place.* In 2009 he received the Shelley Memorial Award from the Poetry Society of America. He teaches at the University of California Santa Cruz.

PERMISSIONS

David Axelrod: "Word Over All, Beautiful as Sky" from *What Next, Old Knife?* (Lost Horse Press, 2012) and "Behold—This Compost" from *Departing by a Broken Gate* (Wordcraft of Oregon, 2010), used by permission.

Polly Bee: "The Basque Hotel Noriega" used by permission of the author.

William Blake: "Ah! Sun-flower" from *Songs of Innocence and Experience.*

Robert Bly: "Love Poem" from *Silence in the Snowy Fields* (Wesleyan University Press, 1962), used by permission of the author.

Deborah Bogen: "The Migraine's Art" used by permission of the author.

Michelle Boisseau: "Self-Pity's Closet" from *Trembling Air* © 2003 by Michelle Boisseau. Reproduced with the permission of the Louisiana State University Press.

Bonnie Bolling: "The 'C' Word" used by permission of the author.

Jan Bottiglieri: "Five" used by permission of the author.

Brian Brodeur: "Asters" used by permission of the author.

Sharon Bryan: "White Space" from *Sharp Stars* (BOA Editions, 2009), used by permission of the author.

Christopher Buckley: "Drinking Champagne" from *Spectrum,* and "Antiques Road Show" from *Hubbub,* used by permission of the author.

Susanne Buffam: "On Nostalgia" and "On Impediments" used by permission of the author.

Wanda Coleman: "Dear Little Boy" from *African Sleeping Sickness* (Black Sparrow Press, 1990), used by permission.

Robert Creeley: "The Sentence" from *Selected Poems, Robert Creeley* (University of California Press, 1991), used by permission.

Brad Crenshaw: From "Medea" from *My Gargantuan Desire* (Greenhouse Review Press, 2010), used by permsission.

e. e. cummings: "if you like my poems let them," part IV of "Poems for Elaine Orr, 1918-19"; and "it is at moments after I have dreamed," part X of "Sonnets—Unrealities" from *E. E. Cummings: Complete Poems 1904–1962* (Liveright Publishing corporation and W.W. Norton & Company, 1994). Reprinted by permission of W.W. Norton & Company, Inc.

J.V. Cunningham: "Nos. 55 & 76" from *A Century of Epigrams,* appeared in *Poems of J. V. Cunningham* (Swallow Press, 1997), used by permission.

Kate Daniels: "The Writer" from *A Walk in Victoria's Secret* (Louisiana State University Press, 2010), used by permission.

Marsha de la O: "Document Attributed to Goya" used by permission of the author.

Fred Dings: "Mathew 6: 9-13" and "Redwing Blackbirds" from *After the Solstice* (Orchises Press, 1993), used by permission.

Jennifer Kwan Dobbs: "For Gwanghyun's Library" used by permission of the author.

John Donne: "Niobi," from *The Poems of John Donne* (Heritage Press).

John Olivares Espinoza: "Old Man Watching a Child Knock Down Pomegranates During a Fata Magana" and "Ode to My Tío Pepe" used by permission of the author.

Robert Frost: "The Silken Tent" from *The Poetry of Robert Frost* (Holt, Rinehart and Winston, 1969), used by permission.

Jack Gilbert: "The Abandoned Valley," "The Reinvention of Happiness" and "Metier" from *Refusing Heaven; Poems by Jack Gilbert*, used by permission of Alfred A. Knopf, a division of Random House, Inc.

Micahel Hannon: "Magnetic Memo" used by permission of the author.

C. G. Hanzlicek: "Disembarking" used by permission of the author.

James Harms: "You Again?" and "So Long, Sunset Boulevard" used by permission of the author.

Juan Felipe Herrera: "A Yard Sale in Mid-April" used by permission of the author.

Lee Herrick: "Korean Poet in California" used by permission of the author.

Edward Hirsch: "Commuters" from *Wild Gratitude* (Alfred A. Knopf, 1986), used by permission.

Jane Hirshfield: "Sentence" from *After* (HarperCollins, 2006) used by permission of the author.

John Hodgen: "Coming to Grief" used by permission of the author.

Garrett Hongo: "Nostalgic Catalogue" from *The River of Heaven* (Alfred A. Knopf, 1988), used by permission.

Christopher Howell: "Little Spring Poem" and "October in Kansas," used by permission of the author.

T. R. Hummer: "Where You Go When She Sleeps" from *The Angelic Orders* (Louisiana State University Press, 1982), used by permission of the author.

Mark Jarman: "Insomnia" and "Don't Get Your Hopes Up," used by permission of the author.

John Keats: "Bright Star" from *The Complete Poetry and Selected Prose of Keats,* Modern Library.

Stephen Kessler: "Another Birthday Poem" from *Burning Daylight* (Littoral Press, 2007), used by permission of the author.

Christine Kitano: "Cooking Lesson" used by permission of the author.

Bill Knott: "The Final Word," "Don't Get Your Hopes Up" and "Storm: Farmboy Dreaming to Reach the Sea" from *All My Thoughts Are the Same: Collected Short Poems 1960–2010* and "Keys in His Hand" from *Complete Sonnets 1969–2009* used by permission of the author.

Dorianne Laux: "The Thief" from *What We Carry* (BOA Editions, 1994), used by permission.

Carol Lem: "Reading Wang Wei after Meeting with Dr. Wong" used by permission of the author.

Philip Levine: "Daybreak" and "Identity Theft" used by permission of the author.

Larry Levis: "Winter" from an unpublished manuscript, used by permission of the Estate of Larry Levis.

Alexander Long: "Snow Shower with Sun" from *Light Here, Light There* (C & R Press, 2009), used by permission of the author.

Perrie Longo: "Relax, hummingbird . . ." and "The period misses . . ." used by permission of the author.

Suzanne Lummis: "For My Ashes" used by permission of the author.

Antonio Machado: "Every man . . ." translated by Dennis Maloney from *There Is No Road* (White Pine Press, 2003), used by permission.

Derek McKown: "Unrelenting" used by permission of the author.

Joseph Millar: "Breasts" used by permission of the author.

Czesław Miłosz: "Autumn" from *Roadside Dog,* reprinted by permission of Farrar, Straus and Giroux, LLC (1998).

Linda Pastan: "The New Dog" from *The Cortland Review,* used by permission of the author.

Kenneth Rexroth: "January Night" from *The Collected Shorter Poems*, copyright © 1944 by Kenneth Rexroth. Reprinted by permission of New Directions Publishing Corp.

James Richardson: "Only the dead. . ." and " Gravity's reciprocal . . ." from *Interglacial: New and Selected Poems & Aphorisms* (Ausable Press, 2004), used by permission.

Katarina Roberts: "Midway Atoll" and "Chinchorro" used by permission of the author.

Kay Ryan: "Ideal Audience" from the *Niagara River* (Grove Press Poetry, 2005), used by permission.

Dixie Salazar: "Muscatel Sonnet" and "Meteor Showers, Yosemite" used by permission of the author.

Luis Omar Salinas: "Tonight" from *Crazy Gypsy* (Origenes Publication La Raza Studies F.S.C., 1970), used by permission of the estate of Luis Omar Salinas.

Sheila Sanderson: "It So Happens" used by permission of the author.

William Shakespeare: "Sonnet No. 66" from *William Shakespeare: The Sonnets,* Signet Classics.

Timothy Sheehan: "Visitation" from *Here* (Vandenberg Press, 1981), used by permission of the author.

Gary Soto: "Eternity at Zak's Car Wash" used by permission of the author.

Lisa Steinman: "Being Stirred" used by permission of the author.

Gerald Stern: "Aliens," "Against Whistling" and "The Crossing" used by permission of the author.

Joseph Stroud: "During the Rains" from *Of This World: New and Selected Poems* (Copper Canyon Press, 2008), used by permission.

Cole Swensen: "If Land Is the Dream of It," from *Denver Quarterly,* used by permission of the author.

Jie Tian: "Sisters" used by permission of the author.

Rhett Iseman Trull: "If We Still Believed the World Was Flat" from *The Real Warnings* (Anhinga Press, 2009), used by permission.

Amy Uyematsu: "Zen Brush" used by permission of the author.

Jon Veinberg: "The Mad Woman's Harp" used by permission of the author.

Diane Wakoski: "The Cup of Gardenias" used by the permission of the author.

Lauren Watel: "My Love, I Am Here" from *Triquarterly,* used by permission of the author.

Walt Whitman: "The Runner," "A Farm Picture," "Out of the Cradle Endlessly Rocking," from *Leaves of Grass,* Modern Library.

William Carlos Williams: "The Great Figure" and "The Red Wheelbarrow" from *The Collected Poems: Volume I, 1909-1939,* copyright ©1938 Reprinted by permission of New Directions Publishing Corp.

Paul Willis: "For the Good of the Cause" used by permission of the author.

Donald Wolff: "The Odds" and "More Please" used by permission of the author.

Charles Wright: "Scalp Mountain," "Remembering San Remo" and "Death" from *China Trace* (Wesleyan University Press, 1977), used by permission of the author.

W. B. Yeats: "When You Are Old" from *The Collected Poems of W. B. Yeats.*

David Young: "Ohio" from *Seasoning: A Poet's Year* (Ohio State University Press), and in *Field of Light and Shadow: Selected and New Poems* (Knopf, 2010), used by permission.

Gary Young: "I would live forever" and "The signature mark of autumn" from *Even So: New and Selected Poems* (White Pine Press, 2012); "That winter" from *No Other Life* (Heyday Books, 2005), used by permission.